# Wisdom

# Wisdom

## (A Cryptic Comparison of Thoughts of Some Philosophies and 444 Points to Ponder on Important Contemporary Issues Primarily Relevant to India)

Dr Adhikarla S. Rao

GenNext Publication

First Published, 2018

*Published by*

GenNext Publication
5, Ansari Road
Daryaganj, New Delhi-110002
Phone: 9811692060
E-mail: gennextpublication@hotmail.com

*Printed at:* G. Print Process, Delhi.

**Cataloging in Publication Data—DK**
Courtesy: D.K. Agencies (P) Ltd. <docinfo@dkagencies.com>

**Rao, Adhikarla S., author.**
Wisdom : a cryptic comparison of thoughts of some philosophies and 444 points to ponder on important contemporary issues primarily relevant to India / Dr Adhikarla S. Rao.
pages cm
Includes text in Hindi and Sanskrit (Sanskrit in roman also).

ISBN: 978-93-5324-124-7

1. Philosophy, Indic. 2. Social problems—India—Philosophy. I. Title.

LCC B131.R36 2018 | DDC 181.4 23

# Contents

# Foreword

Buddhism, Jainism and Sikhism are all India born religions which have many elements and vocabulary of Hinduism. Further, every religion has a big list of beliefs and "do's and don'ts". Dr. Rao, in his small book has laid out many vital principles which are unique and uniquely stated to their respective religions.

As I know intimately the contents of his three books, all published by Kalpaz Publishers New Delhi, I have no hesitation in recommending this book. His two books namely "Thoughts on Higher education and a brief Introduction to Holy Quraan" are highly useful to readers in the context of the present book. Uniqueness of this book is conciseness and appraisal of a variety of issues in the form of small points and targeting readers from wide backgrounds, primarily in an Indian context.

I am confident that this small book will create a large awareness among many.

**Professor Dr P. Tauro,**
**PhD (Wisconsin)**

Former Professor of Eminence &
Dean Post -Graduate Studies (Rtd)
HAU, Hisar-125004 (Haryana)

# Preface

**Dear Readers,**

The book is given the title "WISDOM" keeping in view the contents and the objective of the book and its meaning as explained by "Reader's Digest Great Dictionary". As per the Dcitionary wisdom can be meant as the ability to take actions or decisions based on the body of knowledge and experience.

Our country is highly heterogenous in terms of so many parameters and has a long way to become a power to reckon with. If not exactly the same situation with many other countries particularly under devleoped and developing also have a long way to go. There had been many conflicts in the past and there can be many in future too. It is not posible to predict the nature and magnitude of problems which any society/ country can face. So future is not free from all sorts of fear and anxiety. Hence there is a need for people to become philosophical to cope up with the miseries of life besides being practical too and taking the necessary efforts.

In view of the above a cryptic overview of some philosphies has been given along with 444 opinions/ comments. The opinions/comments broadly fall under Economics, Philosophy, History, Sociology, Education and Science & Technology, Politics, Human Relations, Quotes and Quips pertaining to different topics. Though the points have been mentioned keeping our country in mind, many of them can find applicability to other countries too.

Opinions/comments are made both in a formal way and also in a lighter vein. No offense is meant. Reading and reflecting over the contents would definitely and considerably improve your understanding about men and matters in a very short time. A countable comments were repeated for emphasis with a different shade of opinion/combination of words. There are genuine conflicting views on so many issues and they can be resolved only by viewing the matter from different angles.

This small book will cater to the needs of a large and wider audience from different age groups and educational backgrounds. It would enrich your General Knowledge and will help you to build up your own opinions and help you to acquire "wisdom" as explained above and participate in nation's building.

Your feedback may be mailed to adhikarla@gmail.com

# Acknowledgement

I sincerely thank Mr. Anil Kumar, PhD student for sparing his computer for my work. Further I also think him and two more PhD students, Mr. G. Sathish Kumar and Mr. Ravi Bharadwaj for helping me in the formatting of my book on the computer.

# Part - I

# Cryptic Comparision of Thoughts of Some Philosophies

## A. Some Analogies in Advaita Philosophy ( अद्वैत सिद्धांत )

An understanding and appreciation of Advaita Philosophy (Philosophy of Non-Dualism) is recommended for one to be really secular which is the need always for our country. I have quoted all major analogies.

I hope constantly reflecting on these analogies may help one to come out with new ones which could be refreshingly pedantic and pedagogic to the demanding modern audience.

1. When we do not have a correct knowledge, we do fail to recognise a rope as a rope but perceive it as a snake. Similarly lack of knowledge of Brahman (ब्रह्म), which is of the form of consciousness, leads to the perception of the consciousness as the universe.
2. All ornaments made of gold are in essence only gold always. Similarly, all objects born of Brahman are in essence only Brahman always.
3. The way deluded think a rope as a snake, nacre as a silver, mud as a pot, thread as a cloth, gold as an ear ring, water as a wave, branchless tree trunk as a person during night, mirage as water, wood as house,

iron as sword, similarly the ignorant person has inferred the atman (soul/आत्मा) as the body.

4. The way we falsely imagine blue colour in the sky which has no form and is void, similarly we falsely imagine this entire universe in Brahman.
5. In waves and in tides it is the water that expresses itself. Similarly it is the copper that expresses itself in different copper vessels. In the same manner in all that appears in the universe, it is the Brahman that expresses itself.
6. The way clay, being in a particular form is named and construed as pot and thread as a cloth, Brahman is being understood as the universe. Pot is just a name given to clay in a particular form. It is so with the name "cloth". When the name and form is dropped off only "clay" and 'thread" remains. Similarly drop off the names and forms in the universe and know the Brahman.
7. The way we tend to perceive that the tree is inverted on seeing its reflectance in a stream of water; that the trees and other objects on the river banks as moving while travelling in a boat; the way we perceive even white objects as yellow when suffering from jaundice; the way all objects appear as revolving when we are giddy; the way we think of sun looking at the circular glow of fast moving fire stick; the way big trees at a distance appear as small saplings and small objects appear as big when we view through a magnifying glass; the way we see due to illusion created by sun rays a, water on a glassy surface and vice versa; fire in the jewel and jewel in the fire; the way moon appears moving while the clouds are moving in the sky; the way man is confused about the directions in which he has to go in a foreign land; in the same manner (i.e. as mentioned in the above

examples) man is falsely perceiving Atman as body (i.e. a body in the atman) due to the influence of ignorance.

8. It is the same moon that gets reflected in an undisturbed pool of water, in waves and also in whirlpool of water. Yet we falsely imagine that moon is moving in waves and whirlpool as the reflected image appears moving in them.

9. Sea water after getting processed give us salt in a solidified form. The same salt if dissolved back into sea water loses its name and form. Similarly, a realised soul loses his name and form and dissolves into Brahman.

10. Sun gets reflected in different waters, and may appear stable or unstable, clean or unclean depending on the nature and state of water. In fact the sun is unaffected and remains shining with its natural splendour. Similarly Brahman though appearing in different ways because of its association with different adjuncts, remains unaffected and shines forth in accordance with its real nature.

11. It is the inherent nature of the sun to shine, water to be cold and fire to be hot. Similarly, truth, consciousness, bliss, permanency and purity are the inherent properties of Atman.

12. This universe consisting of so many objects with different names and forms is like a city reflected in a mirror. The way for a dreamer all the objects appear to be outside, though they are actually arising from within, all objects of this universe are just a projection of one's own mind.

Peace Peace Peace (Om Shanti Om Shanti Om Shanti)

## B. Glimpse of Saint Kabir ( संत कबीर ) with Comparisons of Quotes of other Philosophers

Thoughts of Kabir mentioned here is from a small book containing 1008 verses, by Manoj Publications (2007), Delhi, entitled Kabir Vaani-Satya Gyanamrith (कबीर वाणीं सत्य–ज्ञानामृत). Verses are in Avadhi (a dialect of Hindi) and the explanation in Hindi.

Both Hindus and Muslims accept as well as reject him and Kabir also criticised both Hinduism and Islam. He opposed casteism, rituals, fake gurus.

Many Hindus wrongly quote Kabir saying that he has used the word "Rama (राम)" but he does not refer to Lord Rama of Ayodhya but the indwelling Soul i.e. "Atma ram" or "Antaryami (अंतर्यामी)". By saying "Ram rasayan' (राम रसायन) he means Gyan (ज्ञान). So it is a wrong notion to say that Kabir has praised or mentioned Rama in his philosophy. Similar when he uses the word "Hari darshan" (हरि दर्शन) or "Hari milan" (हरी मिलन, he means only the indwelling soul.

Kabir's message or philosophy is simple. "You have to realise the indwelling soul (Atma sakshatkaar/आत्मा साक्षात्कार). This is possible only by receiving instruction (Upadesh उपदेश) from a "Sadguru (सद्‌गुरु)" (not Guru but Sadguru i.e. true preceptor. Because Gurus are many but Sadgurus are few or only one may be there whom you should be fortunate enough to meet.

Sometimes, he uses the word Poorn Sadguru (पूर्ण सद्‌गुरु) i.e. complete preceptor. After that one has to practice what Sadguru has instructed. There is no other way for salvation". This message he tries to explain by numerous similes, allegories, symbolisms, comparisons and contrasts etc. "There is no way out except Sadguru". Now we are in a fix! How to find out our Sadguru? Where is He? Is there only one Sadguru for all the 134 crore plus population of India? Or there are many? It appears there are only a few as Kabir says. The way oceans are large but pearls are found, real saints are few. Adi Shankaracharya (आदि शंकराचार्य) said "Mahapurusha samshrayam (महापुरुष संश्रय:)" i.e. getting to meet a Sadguru and that is possible only by Gods grace. Kabir says when your virtuous deeds mature, you bump into a Sadguru. In case you have firm faith and deep conviction, you would come across a Sadguru.

There can also be some confusion whether he has preached Advaita (philosophy of Non-dualism) or Dvaita (philosophy of dualism—(द्वैत सिद्धांत). Give below are a few similes and sayings of Kabir. In the following, whenever the term "Guru" comes it means "Sadguru".

1. Renounce ego to overcome MAYA (Illusions-माया). Guru can bestow on you the right path and attitude. Of course he can be—not necessarily—a stern disciplinarian which you have to bear with. Till true knowledge (i.e.Gyan) dawns, it is impossible to be free from the shackles of worldliness (samsara—संसार). If you do not realise yourself you will be reborn and dying again and again. Kabir seems to believe in rebirth. Abrahamic religions do not believe in rebirth. (Bhav saagar ke jaal me fus kar baar baar doobthey marthey rahengey—भव सागर के जाल में फस कर डूबते मरते रहेंगे). Mere idol worship or pilgrimage is of no use nor fake gurus. Only Sadguru and the company of saints and sages (satsang—सत्संग). Shun the company of Kusang or Nigurey (bad people—(कुसंग, निगुरे) however rich and even charitable they are. Do not bother if you are presently a bad man. You can even now approach a Sadguru and he will accept you and show the path of salvation. "Guru guru me bhed hai guru guru me bhav—गुरु गुरु में भेद है गुरु में भाव" Gurus differ widely in their knowledge and practices and beliefs. Therefore you have to select only true guru सच्चा गुरु who can free you from the

illusion of the world and can lead you to liberation by teaching you the real "word" i.e. the word on which one has to reflect. This statement is puzzling because in bible also such a quotation is there. "In the beginning was the word, the word was with the God and the word was God". So we cannot know what this means unless and until we approach the guru and take his instruction. In case you happen to select a less qualified guru then you have only half baked knowledge and with this neither you can earn your bread nor can attain liberation. Such people start wearing saffron robes (Bhagave kapade—भगवे कपड़े) and start begging at every house. Kabir is highly opposed to this simple begging and he insists to do some work. Kabir like Hindus believes in 64 branches of knowledge (चौसठ कला) but these branches cannot lead you to liberation and Hindus call them as "Apara vidya" (secular arts or branches of knowledge) and the knowledge leading to liberation as "Para vidya" (supreme knowledge).

2. (Nigura brahman nahi bhala, gurumukh bhala chamaar— निगुरा ब्राह्मण नहीं भला, गुरमुख भला चमार. Knowledgeable cobbler is better than an ignorant Brahmin. This type of episode is there in Hindu mythology where a Brahmin goes to a butcher to get knowledge -"Vyadha geetha—व्यध गीता". Sadhu though lives in the world is not affected by the world. Stars and moon get reflected in the same water where fishes also are there. But stars and moon are not living with fishes.

Today unfortunately we talk about so many Swamijis / Gurus (saints) landing in trouble and controversy. Kabir says in Kaliyug, it is inevitable and only fake saints get respect and worship and true saints are not recognised. (Kaamuk, krodhi thatha chanchal manke dhingi logonki seva, pooja ho rahi hai. Chaal bagule ki chalthey hai magar apne aapko hans kahlathe hai, Simh ka vesh dharan karke bhed ki chaal chalthey hai—कामुक क्रोधी धधा चंचल मनके धिंगी लोगों की सेवा पूरा हो रही है मगर अपने आपको हंस कहलाते है). One whose appearance is different from their actions, or speak something and do something else. How they can give you Gyan (True knowledge) ?? Tiruvalluvar (ancient Tamil philosopher) also mentioned that there are many people in this world of the type "Vinay veru chol veru pattar thodarpu" i.e. their actions are different and what they speak/ preach is different) . These fake gurus may have a shaven head, a rosary, saffron robes and a naamam (Tilak—तिलक on forehead) but without any true devotion. Adi Shankaracharya said similarly in the hymn "Bhaja Govindam" "jatilo mundi lunchitha keshaha kashayambhara bahukrutha veshaha (जटिलो मुंडी लुन्धित केश: कशायाम्बरा बहुक्रुता वेश:)............udara nimithham bahu krutha veshaha (उदर निमित्तं बहुक्रुता वेश:)." (i.e. so many morphological appearances resembling a saint are displayed only to fill the stomach /earn the bread. "Tan ko jogi sab kare man ko kare na koyee (तन को जोगी सब करे मन को करे न कोई)" i.e. everyone tries to make the body clean but not the mind/heart. When a person is too bad he is like a snake coiling around a sandal wood tree. Even then it cannot get the smell of sandal (चन्दन). It is not the fault of the sandal wood true as the snake is full of poison. In the same way, when too bad a man even if he does Satsang सत्संग, congregational prayer) with saints etc he would not be changed. (But the approach of even too bad man also towards good/God is approved by Lord Krishna in Geetha) and at some places by Kabir too. (Opposite of Satsangi (good company) is Kusangi (bad company) . The way you cannot cross a river sitting on a stone, you cannot cross the river of life by associating with kusangi. It is a belief that during the star of swaati स्वाति नक्षत्र a drop of water falling in a sea shell (सीप) becomes a pearl but the same drop falling in the mouth of a snake becomes poison. Hence, depending on the association the properties of a matter or men change. (saadhu santh samudr ke samaan hai aur sadguru den swaathi nakshatr ki boondh ke samaan hai—साधू संत समुद्र के सामान है और सद्गुरु धेन स्वाति नक्षत्र की बूँद के सामान है)

3. Kabir used the words like Prem, Premi, viraha etc with respect to sadguru. (premi doondath my phiroon, premi miley na koyee .Premi se premi mile vish se amruth hoi –प्रेमी ढून्दत मे फिरूँ, प्रेमी मिले न कोई, प्रेमी से प्रेमी मिले विष से अमृत होई) I, a true seeker keep wandering in search of a true Guru and if a true seeker happens to meet a true Guru even poison can become nectar) .

Realised souls does not care for the body. Time can destroy the body but not the knowledge of self. Remembering God is easy and this is enough to attain him or realise oneself. (raathon pehar sumiran karthey raho—रातों पहर सुमिरन करते रहो). Kabir at only few places uses the word God and most of the places uses the word sadguru. Both statements converge. If you pray God he will direct you to sadguru and subsequently you realise yourself. The pithy Greek sentence "Know thy self" sums up Kabir's philosophy. This knowing of self is possible either through God or through sadguru. (Dukh me sumiran sab karey, sukh me karena koyee. Sukh me sumiran kare tho dukh kaaheko hoe—दु:ख में सुमिरन सब करे, सुख में करे न कोई, सुख में सिमरन सब करे दु:ख काहे को होए— Everyone remembers God in distress but never when being happy. If one remembers God even when one is happy then there will be no distress) Sumiran (remembering God) should be done always and if you stop your mind may once again get lost. (antarmukhi sada sukhi — अन्तर्मुखी सदा सुखी. One whose senses are introvert is always happy). Similar idea in kathopanishad, Nachiketha was told by Lord Yama यम देव).

4. Jaise karm karoge vaise hi phal paavogey जैसे कर्म करोगे वैसे फल पावोगे (You reap what you sow i.e. your deed determine your fruits, though not necessarily in the same life) . Since many are doubtful of rebirth they do not give much weight age to this saying. Their motto is now or never. Of course in other religions "The day of judgment is there though not rebirth. Do good to others even if they do harm to you. As

Saint Tiruvalluvar says (32/314-Inna cheyidhharai orutthal avarnaan nannayan cheyidhu vidal—If one doés harm, do in return good to them. Jesus Christ went ahead. If someone slaps you on one cheek turn the other cheek.

You do not know when you kick the bucket (die). Death is hovering around you. So do good as early as possible. Share whatever you can with others, knowledge, wealth, food etc. Have a sweet tongue. One adhikaram (a chapter of ten verses in Tirukkural) is there on this aspect entitled "Cholvanmai" ($65^{th}$ chapter). Get initiation from sadguru at the earliest. Ultimately you have to leave with empty hands however stinking rich. Like Hinduism Kabir also believes that you can be reborn in any of the animal species when you will be deprived of knowledge and of doing good to anybody. A human birth is a prerequisite for salvation.

5. Do not be proud of your personality, youth, wealth mansions etc. time will devour every thing and you will be laid on a pyre or buried and subsequently grass will grow on that place which will be grazed by the animals. (maa kuru dhana jana yavvana garvam harathi nimesha kaala sarvam bhajagovindam; मा कुरु धन जन याव्ना गर्व हारती निमेष काला सर्व – शंकराचार्य hymn from Bhaja Govindam composition.Do not be proud of your youth, wealth and following etc. All these can be wiped out in a moment). We are like those flowers which bloom for a while and fall off. Another parallel of Adishankaracharya which Kabir told is, the way we dream and wake up to know it is not real, similarly we are immersed in this illusory world when once we wake up from this, then we realise there is nothing to or take form this world. This whole world is illusory.

The vast majority of people are ignorant of their divine nature. All pervading God inside you is indestructible. This Kabir calls as RAM (राम) i.e. the indwelling supreme as RAM. (Swami Vivekananda said every soul is potential divine and the ultimate aim is to manifest this divinity). The way if there is no fence to a farm and there is access is given to wild beasts, they will eat away all the harvest. Similarly you should construct a fence of knowledge & discrimination and do not allow any access to wild beasts of lust etc which may eat away your actual harvest which is service, good company and devotion. Impermanence of the body Kabir has emphasised in many verses. For e.g. He compares the five pranas (पञ्च प्राण) with five birds and one day a hunter will take away all these i.e. death or time or in other words soul will leave. When you know so well that death is certain why don't you realise yourself before that? Life is like a water bubble which disappears even with a little wind. After death this body would become invisible. Night time is lost in sleep, day time is lost in eating, drinking etc. So we lose lot of life without doing service, devotion and acquiring knowledge to liberate form the world. Hence act fast. You nourish this body like an animal and in this process you forget your divine nature and land in hell. Don't become lazy or dreaming about future and stop working. We do not know what is in store for future. Overcoming time and death is not possible without gaining knowledge from Sadguru.

Kabir was mostly emphasising Sadguru rather than God. For him God is within everyone and sadguru who knows how to realise it can tell you the path for that.

6. Soil tells to the potter. Do not be proud of handling me in any manner. One day I will make you so. You are too much lost in pursuing worldly things and rearing your family and in the end you lose everything worthwhile. You lose both the worlds. "na samsaarik karmon se nipat paaye, nahi paramatma saadhana" "man sey chaahey guru ki seva - bhakthi karo ya samsaarik vishay bhogon ki kamay karo"—न संसारिक कर्मों से निपट पाए, न ही परमात्मा साधना, मन से चाहे गुरु की सेवा, भक्ति करो या स्मसरिक विषय भोगों की कमाय करो। Otherwise you lose both the worlds! (yah tan kaacha kumbh hai—यह तन कच्चा कुम्भ है. This body is like a moist pot it can break at any

time) Quintessence of Kabir's philosophy is Sadguru (True Guru/Teacher, sumiran (सुमिरन) remembering the name of God, satsang (सत्संग) association with the good company & Congregational prayers), seva (सेवा - service) is required to realise the inner self -the God or antaryami. Kabir takes a dig at rich people (ujal pahine kaapda, paan supaari khaay, kabir, guru ki bhakthi bin bhandha jampur jaay.- उजल पहिने कापड़ा पान सुपारी खाय, कबीर, गुरु की भक्ति बिन बंधा जम पुर जाये. You wear shining and attractive clothes and chew paan (पान, betel leaves with nut powder and other ingredients), but this exhibitionism is a waste. Without devotion & service to Sadguru you are bound to be lost in worldly pleasures and ultimately end in yam lok यम लोक-where the Lord of death resides) and hell- नरक). (Adi Shankaracharya has in a nutshell he highlighted the importance of satsang in bhaja govindam - satsangathve nissangtvam nissangatve nirmohatvam, nirmohatvame nischala chittham, nischalachithhamey jeevan mukthi hi सत्संगात्वे निस्संगात्वं निस्संगात्वे निर्मोहत्वं निर्मोहत्वमे निस्चल चित्तं निस्चल चित्तमे जीवन मुकतिः)—association with holy makes you detached and detachment leads to lack of infatuation/desire and lack of infatuation/desire makes you of a firm mind and liberation is nothing but to remain in a state of firm mind always) .

7. All those who used to sleep in posh houses with perfumes on the bodies have disappeared with time and now grass grows on the spot where they have been reduced to ashes. This body is like someone else's house where you cannot stay forever but leave at the earliest & during this do as much good as possible. Feelings of thine and mine is a rope around the neck of ignorant. Only those with Sadguru can be free from this rope and they have the prop of knowledge imparted by Sadguru. Who goes to hell does not depends on whether you are a prince or a pauper. Who does good is saved and others are doomed. Learn from the trees

which were once lush green but now reduced to dry log of woods and now used for fuel. This body is like a lamp which is burning because of the indwelling soul. When this leaves the lamp is extinguished. Knowing this, approach Sadguru, take his blessings and start following what he said at the earliest. Sporting a beard is only a deception without having initiated by a Sadguru. (jhootha sab samsaar hai, kovu na apna meeth.-झूठा सब संसार है कोवू न अपना मीत) This world is full of deceit and an illusion where none is your friend except your indwelling self. Hence try to know thy self) . As a song goes "Maatha, pitha, bandhu, mitr (माता, पिता बंधू मित्र) all will go one by one. Thoo kyon rahega akela (तू क्यों रहेगा अकेला) - Thoo bhi jaayega thera bhi jaayega (तु भी जाएगा तेरा भी जायेगा) ....i.e Mother, father, relatives, friends all will leave you with time. Do you remain alone? No. Even you and all of yours will get lost. Keep this in mind." After ruining your life there is no point in regretting. It can be too late. Jab thak indriya sathathe rahengey koyee chain nahin hai (जब तक इन्द्रीय सताते रहेंगे कोई चैन नहीं है) —As long as the senses are troubling you there can never be any piece to you).

8. Life is short and you have been witnessing so many people leaving all their assets and kicking the bucket i.e. die. Having observed all these why do you want to work and mint money? This world is like a dream i.e. unreal. So do not waste precious time. That man has no fear of death who has subdued his body consciousness, desire and the feeling of mine. Don't forget that you are the indestructible self which is equivalent to almighty Narayana (नारायण). The body is an inert thing which can be reduced to dust in no time.. (Swami Vivekananda used to address "you are the immortal souls") . Sant santoshi sarvada (संत संतोषी सर्वदा i.e. saints are always happy because they know shabad or also pronounced as shabd (the true word) . As to what is this, there is lot of confusion and is not clearly explained. They say it has to be imparted by Guru. In Bible also such a quote is there. In the

beginning was the word, the word was with the God and the word was God. So one has to ask a Christian as to what it means. He told about no unnecessarily speaking ill of others. On this also there is an adhikaram (chapter of ten verses by Saint Thiruvalluvar "inchol" (Sweet speech/tongue) . One quote is "theeyi naal chutta pun ul aarum, aaradhe naavinaal chuttavadu"—A wound burnt by fire can heal but not a wound caused by an harsh tongue (kabhi bhi kadve vachan math bolo, sheethal vachnonko samjho, parkho thatha unhi ka uchcharan prayog karo (कभी भी कडवे वचन मत बोलो, शीतल वाचनों को समझो, परखो थधा उन्हीं का उच्चारण करो)—Don't speak bitter words. Understand and keep speaking only those words which are pleasant.

You should be the same in thought, word and deed. Even if obstacles and sufferings come in your way, keep patience and shed ego which is a poison. As a kural (verse 115) (Text of Saint Thiruvalluvar) says "kedum perukkamum ill alla nenjetthu kodamai chanrorku ani" i.e. loss and gain do not happen without a cause, knowing this one should not be too much disturbed. Geetha also say a lot about being free form the pairs of opposites (Dwandhatheetham (द्वंधों से अतीत) — remaining beyond the pairs of opposites).

9. Khod khad dharthi sahey, kaat koot ban sahey (खोद खाद धरती सहे, काट कूट बन सहे — you till the land with all machinery it will tolerate, similarly the tress which are cut. In the same manner though not ordinary man, a saint can tolerate ill spoken words. Kural verse 151, (agalwarai thaangum nilam pol thammai igal war porutthhal thalai—Just like the earth which supports the men who dif it, men of virtue bear with those who heap scorn on them. The next kural 152 says "poruthhal irappanai enrum adhanay marathhil adhi neenum nanru-Bear with reproach even when you can retaliate; but to forget it will be still better than that).

When you speak well you also become happy (auran ko sheethal kare aapan ko sukh hoi (औरन को शीतल करे आपण को सुख होई). For this He makes a simile a cuckoo with its sweet voice attracts every one while a crow with its sound no one likes.

Prathakaal soorya ke uday hothe hi raathi ka andhakaar nasht hojaatha hai (i.e प्रातकाल सूर्य के उदय होते ही राती का अंधकार नष्ट हो जाता है) as the sun rises darkness of the night disappears. In the same way when you realise yourself (aathmagyaan-आत्मज्ञान) ignorance is destroyed and you no more wander hither and thither losing yourself. Kabir say all the rituals and mantras and tantras etc are false " janthr manthr sab jhoot hai" (जन्तर मंतर सब झूठ है).

10. Swarath ko swarath miley padi padi lumba boomb........maya ku maya mile kar kar lambe haath (स्वार्थ को स्वार्थ मिले पड़ी पड़ी लम्बा बूमब....माया कु माया मिले कर कर लम्बे हात. Two selfish people with open arms only to get their works done. They may desert you when you are in need. Selfless are the true saints. "parmaarthi paropkaari; maroon par maangu nahin apne tan ke kaaj. Parmaarthi maarg ka anusaran karo" (परमार्थी परोपकारी, मरूं पर मांगू नहीं अपने तन के काज, परमार्थी मार्ग का अनुसरण करो); "Dhan rahey na joban rahey, rahey na gaanv na tthanv" ...karide kisi ka kaam. "(धन रहे न जोबन रहे, रहे न गाँव न ठांव, करीदे किसी का काम) When you die nothing remains. What remains is the name and fame earned by your good deeds. Soul is like a bird and the body a cage. When the bird leaves there is no more need of cage. Prolonging of death will only make you enter ripe old age when your faculties are almost at a very low level. At least now try to get in touch with saints and sages. (Remember Adi shankaracharya's .....nahin nahin rakshathi dukrunya karane (न ही न ही रक्षति डुकृङ्करणे), bhajagovindam moodhamathey भज गोविन्दं मूढमते) — when death is approaching

your secular/worldly knowledge does not save you. So keep remembering God. Angam galitham palitham mundam dasan viheenamjaatham trundam thadhapina muchyat aasha pindam (अङ्गं गलितं पलितं मुण्डं दशनविहीनं जातं तुण्डम्, वृद्धो याति गृहीत्वा दण्डं तदपि न मुञ्चत्याशापिण्डम्) Even when all the body deteriorates the desire still persists) Desire is very strong Buddha said it is the root cause of all evils. Kural verses 347 & 350 says the same thing. "patri vidaava idumbai gal patruka patri vidaava thavarku" "pattruka paattatraan pattrinai appatrai patruka patru vidarku" (Sorrows will never let to their hold of those who give not up their hold of desire. Desire the desire of Him who is without desire, in order to renounce desire, desire that desire) . .Two enemies of man are old age and time. How long you can be saved from them. Time is like a thief in dark. It can attack at any time. Samshaya poorni jeevan me shaanthi nahin hothi (संशय पूर्णी जीवन में शांति नहीं होती i.e. a life of uncertainty /doubts has no peace of mind. Time is to be feared and more than the time ignorance is to be feared. Only those who have received initiation from a Sadguru can conquer time (काल), maya (माया), moham (मोह) etc. The new emerging leaves started laughing at the old leaves which have fallen. Old leaves replied; we have completed our life and going. A day will come when you will also fall like us. So don't be stupid and laugh at us. Even the three lords and all demi gods are afraid of time. Then why you are foolish to ignore it? Kaalo jagadbakshaha कालो जगत भक्षः i.e. time devours the whole world. Mind is like a wild elephant. You have to keep on pricking it with ankush (अंकुश, the long pointed iron rod used to control elephants) Only spiritual practices can stop the waywardness of the mind. "man jeethey tho jag jeethey" (मन जीते तो जग जीते i.e if you can conquer the mind you can conquer the world. In this mind are unending waves. The way there are unlimited waves in the ocean as many are thoughts in the mind. Only when you calm it down, knowledge dawns on you. It is a natural tendency of the senses to turn towards objects of pleasure (kathopanishad). Try to completely extinguish this tendency. Then you would realise yourself. This body is like a paper ship. How it can with stand the floods of this worldly desires. Over and above that the five senses are putting pressure to sink it. Hence only when the senses are under control you can cross this world and attain salvation. Mind is the greatest thief, making you to take rebirths. Hence beware and carry out spiritual practices.

11. Get rid of Maya, Moh. Otherwise there can be clashes even among the members of the family. "maya deepak nar pathanga, brhami brahmi maahi paranth (माया दीपक नर पतंगा, ब्रह्मी ब्रह्मी माहि परंत. Maya is like the light of the flame and ignorant man is like the insect which is attracted into the flame and dies in it. Only those who have followed Sadgurus instructions and do devotion & practices can avoid this maya. How bad wealth can be Kabir says "Guru ko chela bish de, pooth pitha ko marsi (गुरु को विष दे, पूत पिता को मर्सी i.e for the sake of wealth a disciple can give poison to his guru and a son can kill his father. Kural, verse 39 says "arrathaal varuvadhe inbam, mattrellam purathha pugalam ila'—What you earn earnestly brings peace the rest is without praise and a waste.

In English it is said man is the most amorous animal. There has been some evolutionary blunder in the evolution of man as far as his reproductive system is concerned. Kabir says kaami kuthha thees din....... kaami nar kuthha sadha, cheha ruthu baraha maas" (कामी कुत्ता तीस दिन....कामी नर कुत्ता सदा, छह रुतु बारह मास i.e. an animal comes to heat once in a way whereas the man is lusty 24 × 7 × 365 throughout the life in this regard. Kaami lajja na karey, man maahi ahlaad, neendh na maangagi saathra, bhook na maangai swaad" (कामी लज्जा न करे, मन माहि अह्लाद, नींद न मांगे साथरा, भूक न मांगे स्वाद) i.e. the way you do not bother about the nature of the bed when you are over taken by sleep and the way you do not bother about the taste of the food when you are too hungry, in the same way the lustful man has no shame of anything. (telugu- Nidhra sukham erugadhu, aakali ruchi erugadhu-When one is overtaken by sleep it does not matter for him whether it is a hard or soft bed. Such pleasure does not influence then.Similarly hunger does not bother about taste)...Sanskrit- kama turaanam na bhayam na lajja (कामा तुरानाम न भयं न लज्जा —in lust there is neither fear nor shame.) (kaam krodh mad lobh lage ghat mein khaan, kabir, moorakh panditha dono ek samaan" (काम क्रोध मद लोभ लगे घट में खान कबीर, मूरख पंडिता दोनों एक सामान i.e. As long as lust, pride, greed etc the base desires are there in your heart there is no difference between an ignorant and learned. (theen lok ki sampadha kab aavai ghar maahi" (तीन लोक की सम्पदा कब आवै घर माहि i.e. How a greedy man thinks? He wants the wealth of all the three worlds in his house.

12. Apna tho koye nahin, ham kahoo ke naahin, paar pahunchi naav jab, milee sab bichude jahi" अपना तो काहू के नहीं पार पहुंची नाव जब, मिली सब बिछुड़े जाही). i.e. In this world no one is ours and we are no one to anyone. Then why this infatuation? The way in a boat we travel together but after reaching the shore /destination we all get separated. A similar e.g. some one has given that life is a train journey. In the compartment we meet many and talk but everyone gets down and get separated when their respective stations come. Kabir says even if you pray idols you should have a Sadguru with whom you can communicate in distress. Kabir takes a dig. If by praying a small stone idol if you can attain salvation then I prefer to pray a mountain and get salvation quickly and more benefits. Saaligram mey bharosa nahin. (सालिग्राम में भरोसा नहीं) It is a small stone symbolic of Vishnu worshipped by Hindus. But it is broken even by a small pressure. Hence Kabir says how it can give salvation?

"patthar paani ki pooja math karo पत्थर पानी की पूजा मत करो). Saadhu santhon ki sangathi mey jaakar seva karo" साधू संतों की संगती में जाकर सेवा करो). Do not pray stones and water. Approach saints and serve.

13. Pure heart is equivalent to Mecca, Medina and Dwaraka. Kural, verse 34 says manathukkan maachilan aadhal annaitthu aran aakula neera pira" (Keep the mind free from evil thoughts. The rest is superfluous and is only of the nature of sound and fury) . kural, verse 364, 'Thooyamai enbadhu ava vinmayi' (Purity of mind consists of freedom from desire).

Kabir says kaankar pathar jori ke, masjid layee chunay, tha chadi mullaha baang de, bahira huva khuday" (कांकर पाथर जोरी के, मस्जिद लई चुनाय, ता चडी मुल्ला बांग दे, बहिरा हुवा खुदाय) i.e. mosque is made of several stones and Mullah there in a high pitched voice addresses Almighty as if HE is deaf. Neither God is deaf nor is far off. He is in your heart. Going to temple or mosques, pilgrimage, worship, fasting, living on the banks of river etc are too minor things and cannot help in realisation. Only Sadguru (true Teacher) can do that. Just by bathing in river Ganga one cannot get rid of his evil characters. A fish in Ganga however washed it is, its characteristic smell does not disappear, similarly just by bathing in Ganga one cannot get rid of his evil characters.

Kabir denounces caste differentiation saying all are made up of the five elements (pancha bhoothas—five primordial elements Viz; sky (आकाश), fire (अग्नि), air (वायु), earth (पृथ्वी), and water (जल) and are formed and come out in the same manner. Here you may refer to Adishankarascharya's maneesha panchakam. The essence of this hymn is, every body's body is the same and every body's soul is the same. Then what is the difference between a high caste/born or low caste/born?

14 "Gyaan buddhi ke bina har koyee aankh rakhthe huve andhe ke samaan hai" (ज्ञान बुद्धि के बिना हर कोई आँख रकते हुवे अंधे के समान है) Without knowledge you are blind even possessing eyes. Kural verse 393, "kannudayar en pawar katror, mukhatthhu rendu punnudayar kallathavar"i.e. The learned are said to have eyes, but the unlearned have only two sores in their face. This body is always a temple or a mosque because the Almighty soul is within. As you sow you reap is both an English proverb and in Hinduism also. Jaisa karni vaisa bharni (जैसा करनी वैस अभारनी. "Prarabdh pahle bana peechey bana shareer प्रारब्ध पहले बना पीछे बना शरीर. Karma precedes birth. You may go anywhere in the cosmos you cannot escape what the body has to suffer. But a sadguru can see that you cope up with the suffering/prarabdha (the consequences of previous births you have to reap in this birth) without losing peace. Preach and practice the same. If two persons on the right path meet their bondage would increase otherwise it will break. " saanche ko saancha mile, adhika badey sneh, jhoothe ko saancha miley thad dey tootey neh (सांचे को सांचे मिले, अधिका बड़े स्नेह, झूठे को सांचा मिले, ताड दे टूटे नेहा). One should be righteous, forgiving and merciful. Be humble for your own sake. "kural verse 125, Ellarkum nanraal panidal"—Humility is good of every one. The mighty elephant cannot separate sugar mixed with sand but an ant can. Similarly a man who is humble can have the opportunity to meet Sadguru. Meet saints, contemplate on Sadgurus initiation, be humble to cross this world of Samsaara. In case you want to destroy yourself then cultivate ego and the sense of I and mine.

**Peace Peace Peace (Om Shanti Om Shanti Om Shanti)**

### C. An Abstract of the ancient Thirukkural (Tamil) of Saint Thiruvalluvar

Reading through, one really wonders. It appears even

two thousand years back, the society had all the major negative elements of the present day world viz; lust, liquor, gambling, poverty, false ascetics, unscrupulous people etc .

Author prescribes many DO's and DONT's for kings, ministers, ambassadors, servants, doctors, farmers and to common man. He mentions the attributes of a stable kingdom and the ways to deal with enemies and relatives. He has high admiration for farmers and house holders and has repeatedly emphasised humility and sweet tongue.

Kural is not a spiritual text discussing entirely about extra terrestrial matters, but it is a work on ethics for all and discusses numerous aspects pertaining to day to day life. A large portion of it 700 Kurals (aphorisms of just seven words) out of 1330 Kurals pertains to matters pertaining to kings and associates managing the kingdom, which was the system in ancient days. However, all these sayings can be applied/are applicable/have applicability to even the modern world and to the general society.

The author is a strong believer in GOD and the book of kural starts in praise of GOD and strongly advocates HIS worship to avoid the evil effects of the world, to be free from anxiety and to cross the ocean of births (repeated births and deaths).

Author is a strong believer in inexorable fate, extols the importance of rain, acknowledges the virtues of ascetics in particular their mastery over five senses; emphasises the practice of virtues, in particular avoidance of anger, bad tongue, ill will etc to attain peace, pleasure in this world and heaven; extolls the house holder as it is he who sustains the society and the ascetics; emphasises the right bringing up of children.

Authors says: that one should be grateful and ingratitude is a sin. That one should be charitable, benevolent and help should be rendered even unsolicited. That one should be noble enough, not to retaliate even if one can and to maintain evenness of mind in both loss and gain.

That one should not be envious, covetous and stealthy. That one should be free from the sense of 'I' and 'Mine'.

There is a controversy about authors faith whether he is a Hindu, Jain or Buddhist? One of the reasons for this controversy is the author condemning eating meat in very strong words. Even Hinduism approves meat eating except for a small group of people.

Though a larger space is devoted to indicate the importance of wealth and other worldly matters, the author says that ultimately wealth is perishable and virtues are imperishable. Author in ten kurals emphasises the need to abandon desire to attain purity of mind and consequently liberation from rebirth.

In 40 kurals author emphasises the importance of learning and listening to the learned, the perils of remaining unlearned and attributes of the wise/ wisdom. Thiruvalluvar emphasises that the right learning is that which will bestow pleasure not only in this life but for seven future lives. Author gives a practical view point of what wisdom is. Wisdom is to control the waywardness of mind, to be able to make out the truth from the sayings of any one, securing and retaining the friendship of the great, to foresee things, to fear what needs to be feared and adjust to the world. The wise should reflect well before taking up a task, should consider losses and gains and employ suitable methods to accomplish the task.

Tiruvalluvar describes the virtues and attributes of a worthy ruler. In the present system, the voters should keep in mind these qualities when they elect their leader and the persons who contest should possess these qualities to compete.

The ruler should be learned, wise, brave, kind ethical, liberal, fearless and vigilant, wisely manage his wealth and regularly monitor his employees, free from pride, anger greed, lust, carelessness and over indulgence. Author warns that the country without a just king would ruin. The ruler should give access to and protect his people and avoid harsh speech but ready to listen even to bitter words. Ruler should generate wealth and use it for the people and the defense of the country. At more than one place the author emphasises the need for a good army and friends and good defence. The king should secure and retain the friendship of the learned & virtuous and thoroughly screen the credentials of his ministers before appointing him. The king should reflect well and assess his and his allies ability Vis-a Vis enemy before waging a war. He should act after due consideration of an appropriate time and place.

In the modern times it is well realised about the problems of fighting an enemy in their own terrain, in an unknown terrain, in a guerrilla warfare, mountainous terrain, on land in air and on water etc. These ideas are well reflected in the kurals.

In 40 kurals author emphasises the importance of learning and listening to the learned, the perils of remaining unlearned and attributes of the wise/ wisdom. Some of the authors views makes one to remember Raja Bhartruhari's (राजा भर्तृहरि) aphorisms under "vidwat paddhati विद्वत पद्धति), moorkha paddhati (मूर्ख पद्धति), sajjanpaddhati सज्जन पद्धति), ardha paddthati (अर्ध पद्धति) etc. ancient Tamil Saint Tiruvalluvar emphasises that the right learning is that which will bestow pleasure not only in this life but for seven future lives.

Thiruvalluvar gives a practical view point of what wisdom is. Wisdom is to control the waywardness of mind, to be able to make out the truth from the sayings of any one, securing and retaining the friendship of the great, to foresee things, to fear what needs to be feared and adjust to the world. The wise should reflect well before taking up a task, should consider losses and gains and employ suitable methods to accomplish the task.

Thiruvalluvar gives very clear guidelines for choosing a minister (to be read in the present times also as counsellor, advisor, PA, PS , PC (personal office staff) etc) . Advisors should be thoroughly tested for their attitudes towards virtues, wealth and love for pleasure and for their family and a decision taken accordingly weighing the utility of both his merits and demerits. Further the minister should be highly learned, perseverant, firm, committed to people, judicious in the choice of means and loyal. How important loyalty is to a minister is well stated by the author by saying " seventy crore enemies are far better than one bad minister". The minister should be sweet tongued, yet be very effective in communication. He should decide his words after carefully assessing his friends, enemies and others listening to him. Minister should act in ways which bring grace and fame to his fellow men and the king and be judicious in the means by which he wish to enrich the king. A minister should not forego any opportunity to secure the support of foes.

A minister should not be casual in his behaviour while in the presence of a king. Nor he should possess a prying nature. He should give counsel at a right time. Even after having a long familiarity, the minister should not try to take liberty and indulge in unwarranted acts. A minister should be a good face reader. In an assembly a minister should decide to speak & carefully word his speech only after having a clear understanding of the men surrounding him.

One should be firm after deciding to act and avoid undue delay in execution. Neither one take up acts which are likely to end in disaster nor one should get disheartened if an act taken up, even after due deliberation ends in failure. However, one should not on his own abort an action. One should act after due deliberation with respect to time and place, manner of execution, and the resources involved, effort required, likely obstacles to be faced and the ultimate good it is going to bestow.

Similarly, while employing other officers, the king should consider both good and bad, and ascertain the persons ability to increase resources. The person should possess wisdom and clarity of mind and perseverance and should not be stealthy. Personal attachment should not be a criteria in appointment as the person near and dear may not possess the above qualities and hence turn out to be detrimental to the king. An ambassador should be a patriot, possess a thorough knowledge of the nature of his duties and possess a sense of discrimination while communicating.

Author advocates consideration and compassion to kith and kin. He emphasises that sloth, idleness, carelessness, undue delay in any matter and undue sleep are ruinous and hence should be avoided by one who wish to prosper. One should preserve in the midst of troubles and sorrows but should not easily succumb.

Many prescriptions of the present time by modern economists and UN organisations have been prescribed by the author, for a country to flourish. A country should be free from hunger, disease, internal and external enemies. People belonging to different categories should live in harmony among themselves and with the rulers. A country should generate knowledge and wealth and have invincible defence both in terms of arms and army. While highlighting the indispensability of a valiant army, the author warns that the army can function only if its well being is duly taken care of and has befitting generals.

Thiruvalluvar gives enormous importance for friendship and devotes nearly 50 kurals on this topic. Raising some body to a status of a friend has to be a slow process after screening the credentials. A true friend not only shares lighter moments but also chides if need be. He is with you always supporting & making you walk on the right path.

Author cautions that friendship is not mere expressions on the face but what dwells in the heart. Hence though the author recommends to have friends he gave several words of caution. After all this process, when you make a friend dont leave him at any cost. He further says, after following his words of caution and making friends, do not forsake them and to give a benefit of doubt to old friends if something untoward happens because of them.

While duly acknowledging the importance of wealth for living and welfare author cautions as well about the means of acquisition of wealth. Wealth should be earned righteously. Better to live in poverty rather than to amass wealth by sinful means.

Thiruvalluvar uses the word 'fool' both in a practical and philosophical sense. He says that "the suffering that fools inflict upon themselves is hardly possible even to foes". A fool is one who does not shun what ought to be shunned and refrains from pursuing what needs to be pursued. Hence a fool is capable of destroying not only this life but even the future seven lives. Author says one is really a fool who understands and preaches rightly but does not practice accordingly.

Thiruvalluvar points out to "hatred" as the greatest calamity and strongly advocates to avoid hatred to enjoy fame, peace & prosperity by an individual or society. A practical point advocated by the author is "it is too foolish for a man without any support to incur the hatred of many". Author strongly advises to make an agreement with a foe if need be and also try to subdue a foe after ascertaining that the foe is weak. He further says not to reveal your weaknesses to your foes and even to your friends and not to incur the wrath of ministers (मंत्री). More particularly author cautions about internal enemies and says living with internal enemies is like living with cobras in the same house. Author advises not to entertain spouse's interference in the official affairs.

Thiruvalluvar gives three important tips about Nutrition Viz; eat moderately, eat what is agreeable and eat only when the previously taken food has been digested.

Though at one place Thiruvalluvar says that "all are equal at birth, in a separate section he does acknowledge the congenital power in influencing certain qualities like humility, speaking truth, proper behaviour, fear of doing prohibited acts, showing warmth in relations etc. He says that differences in circumstances cannot so easily make the lowly great or vice versa. (After the human genome sequencing the debate of nature versus nurture has again gained momentum).

Thiruvalluvar commends people who value self respect and fight for it till the end. One may overcome by an inferior and one is made to bow to him. This one should face it. Subsequently it may help to avoid the enmity.

To preserve wealth one should be courteous and be in association with the good.. Men should acquire wealth but should not neglect to acquire fame and should not be a miser. Wealth according to author should be enjoyed or donated, otherwise he remains poor though possessing wealth. And such wealth one does not know who will inherit. Author while discouraging begging, criticises the well off for not giving alms with all kindness and advises them to do so.

Thiruvalluvar highly admires the profession of agriculture. He goes to the extent of saying that it is only farmers who really are making a living as all others are dependent on him. Thiruvalluvar has duly appraised the likely consequences of poverty form various angles. He says poverty is the mother of all evils and poverty deprives one not only of this life but future life too. He further says that poverty deprives one of his own kith and kin and if a poor man talks sense he is simply brushed off. Author says that it is very important to understand what wealth is and understand the importance of generation of various goods and services for running the society and thus encourage and respect all.

Unscrupulous people seem to be there even in ancient days. He seems to have been deeply pained and concerned about such people. He condemned them in very strong words. He never considered them as human beings but as those belonging to some other species, who has a striking resemblance to human beings.

It is very common to describe the beauty and various attributes of a woman with moon, sun, stars, sky, different flowers, buds, birds, butterflies, gold, gems, fruits, honey, nectar, fragrances, fishes, deer, arrows, creepers, with the colours of the various objects of nature both animate and inanimate etc.

Both in ancient days and present days, loneliness of spouse because of separation is a harsh fact of life. Men employed in army, men migrating in search of employment, business, greener pastures etc. stay away from their homes and the pain of separation is felt by both the partners. Situations & feelings of such people have been preserved by word of mouth for a long time in different cultures. Women eagerly waiting for their men to return from war is a common feature. One way the partner spends time is by remembering the time spent when they were together. Another way is by dreaming & so on. Men employed in military or other wise away come for a very short time to their homes. Women even while with the partner is simultaneously feeling the pain pondering over about his departure soon and the next meeting would be only after a long gap. During separation, the women feels that nights are long and painful, dreams are both pleasant and troublesome, face becomes pale and loose lustre, the women keeps talking to oneself etc.

When the man lives separated, he wishes that the women should continue to like him And the same wish is there from the women's side too. He says that little anger, skirmishes and pretending dislike all are a part of love. In case the man takes these seriously and tries to keep a distance, the women would really suffer. Women often fears about such a situation. On dislike and pretension between partners the author devotes thirty kurals, as to how each partner feels and expects the other partner to behave, when some dislike is expressed intentionally or unintentionally. The author expects the partners to reconcile at the earliest and restore the warmth and affection. **A few additional points- (Verse numbers are given):**

398- The learning which a man has acquired in one birth, will yield him pleasure in seven births.

406- The unlearned are like worthless barren land; all that can be said of them, is that they exist.

414- Although a man be without learning, let him listen to the teachings of the learned, that will be to him a staff in adversity.

426- To live as the world lives, this is wisdom.

427- The wise are those who know beforehand what will happen; those who do not know this are the unwise.

601- By the darkness of idleness, the indestructible lamp of family will go out and be extinguished.

621- If trouble comes laugh, there is nothing like that to press upon and drive away sorrow.

628- That man never experiences sorrow who does not seek for pleasure and who considers trouble to be natural (to man).

629- He does not suffer sorrow in sorrow, who does not look for pleasure in pleasure.

I wish to end by saying Tirukkural by Saint Tiruvalluvar is a 'must to read' for all. Though original is in Tamil translations in other languages are available.

**Peace Peace Peace (Om Shanti Om Shanti Om Shanti)**

**D. Bhagwad Geetha chalisa (40 verses) - A Study for beginners.**

After the original Hanuman chalisa by Goswami Tulsidas many Chalisa's have cropped up. Mine is one such. It is totally my idea for the benefit of beginners. I have taken two slokas (स्लोक) each from every chapter of geetha (भगवद्गीता) except in 2nd and 18th where I have taken four. Hope some more Geetha chalisas will crop up and even Geetha ashtothara satham (108 verses) for the benefit of learners! Numbers at the beginning of the verse indicate the Chapter and the verse in the text.

1.31-I do not see how any good can come from killing my own kinsmen in the battle, nor can I my dear Krishna desire any subsequent victory, kingdom or happiness.

1-39-With the destruction of the dynasty, the eternal family tradition is vanquished and thus the rest of the family becomes involved in irreligious practices.

2.13-As the embodied soul continually passes, in this body, from boy hood to youth to old age, the soul similarly passes into another body at death. The self realised soul is not bewildered by such change.

2.23-The soul can never be cut into pieces by nay weapon, nor can be burned by fire, nor moistened by water, nor withered by the wind.

2.47-You have a right to perform your prescribed duty, but you are not entitled to the fruits of action. Never consider yourself to be the cause of the result of your activities, and never be attached to not doing your duty.

2.56-One who is not disturbed in spite of three fold miseries, who is not elated when there is happiness, and who is free from attachment, fear and anger, is called a sage of steady mind.

3.14-All living bodies subsist on food grains, which are produced from rains. Rains are produced form by performance of Yagna (यज्ञ) — sacrifice) , and Yagna is born of prescribed duties.

3.21-Whatever action that is performed by a great man, common man will follow in his foot steps. And whatever standards he sets by exemplary acts, all the world pursues.

4.7- Whenever and wherever there is a decline in religious practice, O descendant of Bharatha, and a predominant rise of irreligion-at that time I descend myself.

4.8- In order to deliver the pious and to annihilate the miscreants, as well as to re-establish the principles of religion, I advent myself millennium after millennium.

5.3- One who neither hates nor desires the fruits of his activities he is always renounced. Such a person, liberated from all dualities, easily overcomes the bondage and is completely liberated, O mighty armed Arjuna.

5.18-The humble sage by virtue of true knowledge, sees with equal vision a learned and gentle brahmana (priestly class), a cow, an elephant, a dog and a dog eater.

6.30-For one who sees me everywhere and sees everything in me, I am never lost, nor he is ever lost to me.

6.35-The blessed Lord said: O mighty armed son of Kunti, it is undoubtedly very difficult to curb the restless mind, but is possible by constant practice and by detachment.

7.16- Four kinds of pious men render devotional service unto me-the distressed, the desirer of wealth, the inquisitive, and he who is searching for the knowledge of the Absolute.

7.26- As the supreme personality of God head, I know everything that has happened in the past, all that is happening in the present and all things that are yet to come. I also know all living entities, but me no one knows.

8.5- And whosoever, at the time of death, quits his body, remembering me alone, at once attains my nature. Of this there is no doubt.

8.14- For one who remembers me without deviation, I am very easy to obtain because of his constant engagement in devotional service.

9.22- But those who worship me with devotion, meditating on my transcendental form-to them I carry what they lack and preserve what they have.

9.26- If one offers me with love and devotion a leaf, flower, fruit or water, I will accept it.

10.10- To those who are constantly devoted and worship me with love, I give the understanding by which they can come to me.

10.20- I am the self seated in the heart of all creatures. I am the beginning, the middle and end of all beings.

11.12. If hundreds of thousands of suns rose up at once in to the sky, they might resemble the effulgnece of the supreme person in that universal form (विश्वरूप/विराटरूप).

11.13- Arjuna could see in the universal form of the lord the unlimited expansions of the universe situated in one place although divided into many, many thousands.

12.5- For those whose minds are attached to the unmanifested, impersonal feature of the supreme, advancement is very troublesome (i.e. in other words saying -Advaitic pursuit is difficult) To make progress in that discipline is always difficult to those who are embodied.

12.12- Engage yourself in the cultivation of knowledge. Better than knowledge, however, is meditation and better than meditation is renunciation of the fruits of action for by renunciation one can attain peace of mind.

13.25- The super soul is perceived by some through meditation, by some through cultivation of knowledge, and by others through working without fruitive desire.

13.26- There are those who, although not conversant with spiritual knowledge begin to worship the Supreme Person, upon hearing about Him from others. Because of their tendency to hear form authorities, they also transcend the path of birth and death.

14.5- Material nature consists of three modes-goodness, passion and ignorance. When the living entity comes in contact with the nature, he becomes conditioned by these modes.

14.27- And I am the basis of impersonal Brahman, which is the constitutional position of ultimate happiness, and which is immortal, imperishable and eternal.

15.1- The Blessed Lord said: there is a banyan tree which has its roots upwards and branches down and whose leaves are the vedic hymns. One who knows this tree is the knower of vedas.

15.6- The abode of mine is not illumined by the sun or moon, nor by air/electricity. One who reaches it never returns to this material world.

16.18- Bewildered by false ego, strength, pride, lust and anger the demon becomes envious of the Supreme personality of God Head, who is situated in his own body and in the bodies of others, and blasphemes against the real religion.

16.21- There are three gates leading to the hell-lust, anger and greed. Every sane man should give these up, for they lead to the degradation of the soul.

17.23- From the beginning of creation, the three syllables- om tat sat (ॐ तत सत)-have been used to indicate the supreme absolute truth (Brahman) (self - advaitic). They were uttered by Brahmanas while chanting vedic hymns and during sacrifices for the satisfaction of supreme.

17.25- One should perform, sacrifice, penance and charity, with the word tat.The purpose of such transcendental activities is to get free from the material entanglement.

18.18- Knowledge-, object of the knowledge and the knower are the three factors which motivate the action; the senses, the work and the doer comprise the three fold basis of the action.

18.30- That understanding by which one knows what ought to be done and what ought not to be done, what is to be feared and what is not to be feared, what is binding and what is liberating that understanding is established in the mode of goodness.

18.47- It is better to engage in ones occupation, even though one may perform it imperfectly, than to accept another's occupation and perform it perfectly. Prescribed duties according to ones nature are never affected by sinful reactions.

18.66- Abandon all varieties of religion and surrender unto me. I shall deliver you from all sinful reactions. Do not fear.

**Peace Peace Peace (Om Shanti Om Shanti Om Shanti)**

## E. Fate & Free Will

The topic of free will and fate is a perennial one. No one is convinced about any amount of explanation. How much free will one has? How much is fate? Answers vary form 0-100%

1. Ramana Maharsihi (Tamil nadu) says free will is an ego implanted in the minds of the man. In other words everything is preordained.
2. Rationalists and modern thinkers and even some religions say that man has 100% free will.
3. His holiness Chandrasekhar Bharathi– former Shankaracharya of Sringeri, Karnataka, happened to say that fate and free will are not different. Fate is nothing but free will exercised in the past. What you exercise in the present life is free will. So there is nothing like fate, as fate is simply free will being exercised in the present life. Whether free will exercised in the past can be undone? His holiness says yes. But it depends how much amount of free will you have exercised in the past and how much of free will needs to be exercised now to do or undo a thing. According to the magnitude the answer can be either 'yes' or "no" or "partly/fractionally".

   Only great souls after seeing you, can gauge whether you are in a position to exercise enough free will in the present life and accordingly advice them. Hence ordinary man cannot know whether he can overcome fate or not since he does not have the capacity to know how much free will he has exercised in the past life.

4. If everything is fate then why we are suggested to do atonements ("pariharams"; दोष निवारण) and other "homams" (prescribed rituals, हवन). Obviously to a limited extent we can overcome fate. How much limited is this, we cannot know. The man has to experience it and has to tell. Often an analogy is given. The man's amount free will is compared to that of a bull going around and around tied to an yoke. This is only a qualitative explanation. This should not be inferred to mean that man has limited free will. Because man is committing so many rapes, murders, massacres by bombs, have a stock pile of dangerous weapons which can destroy the world. All these can we say it is limited free will? Why God has given so much of free will to a man that he can do the above. Or it is all because of God's consent? How difficult it is to visualise that rapes, murders, bomb blasts etc all mentioned above can be with Gods consent?

   There are spiritual people who say that fate can be undone 100% by performing appropriate pariharams and homams. At the same time the same spiritualists say that man's problems are due to three factors. viz; Adhyathmika (because of one' s own conduct) adhi bhoudhika (because of other creatures) and Aadi daivika (calamities due to God's intention which is described as his leela लीला, play/sport). Say, natural disasters like earthquakes, floods, cyclones etc.

   Some say that for avoiding Aadhi daivika problems too we have/had mantras (मन्त्र) that need to be chanted regularly and prescribed homams (हवन) to be performed regularly to prevent any future calamity.

But most of this knowledge has been lost according to many.

5. There are many who say this world is created by God for his Sport i.e. Leela. We cannot do much to change the world happenings.
6. There are two common examples in puranas where fate has been avoided.

   The case of Markandeya. He was due for death but Lord Shiva saved him. Here again there are two interpretations. Lord Shiva has saved Markandeya but he has made him to live permanently at his child hood age. So there is no further growth for him i.e. Lord Shiva has frozen him at child hood age. However some say it is not like that. Markandeya had a normal aging process after being saved by Lord Shiva. Another case is that of husband of Sathi Saavithri who had come back to life after preordained death time because of the grace of Lord Yama.
7. It is quite possible, however you may pray, often sufferings cannot be mitigated. For that a palliative answer which is given is, had you not prayed maybe your sufferings would have increased.
8. Theoretically speaking since God is Omnipotent there is nothing which he cannot do or undo. So fate can be overcome if God wants. But the question is how to please God to that extent!?

   **Peace Peace Peace (Om Shanti Om Shanti Om Shanti)**

## F. Bhaja Govindam (भज गोविन्द), hymns of Adi Shankaracharya (आदि शंकराचार्य) and his disciples.

How to begin studying Hindu philosophy in an easy manner? Studying the composition Bhaja Govindam by Adi shankaracharya is one. Dr C. Rajagopala Chari, said that

Adi Shankaracharya has packed into Bhajagovindam, the substance of entire Vedanta (वेदांत).

Bhaja govindam composition consists of 31 verses of four lines each. Out of the 31 only the first 12 have been composed by Adi shankaraacharya together called as Mohamudgaram or dwadasamanjarika stotram. The remaining verses are composed by Adi shankaracharya's disciples.

Bhaja govindam deals with some key human weaknesses and other practical situations and suggests remedies and ultimately the way for salvation.

In the first stanza, adi shankaracharya finding a old man reading a sanksrit grammar book, advises the person that it is unwise to read texts at that age but one should seek God, as at the time of death nothing saves you except worshipping God.

Adi Sankaracharya has used the word "Govinda" for Lord. (Govinda pada was Adi Shankarachaarya's Guru but here the word Govinda means God only. Whether Govinda means Narayana (Lord Vishnu) or not is not clarified by many.

(One may argue what is wrong if one reads secular text books at old age? For e.g. a physicist may read a physics book even at an old age. There are scientists working till advanced age. For them work is worship. However, the message of the stanza is to devote sufficient time to God).

**At what age one should begin concentrating on God?**

**Balastavath kreeda saktha ha., tarunasthavat taruni saktaha, vriddhasthaavat chintha saktaha, Parame Brahmani Kopina sakthaha** (बालस्तावत्क्रीडासक्त: तरुणस्तावत्तरुणीसक्त: वृद्धस्तावच्चिन्तासक्त: परमे ब्रह्मणि कोऽपि न सक्त:)

Child hood is lost in playing, youth is lost in chasing women, Old age is lost in anxiety and worries. Hence the man has not time to devote to God or reflect on Brahman. So the message is start turning towards God as early as possible.

Hindu mythology has examples of child devotees like Dhruva, Markandeya, Prahlada. Hence you have a chance to attain God at an early stage of your life if you turn to God early.

## What is the problem in concentrating on God?

A single word answer is **"DESIRE"**. Lord Buddha after realisation discovered that desire is the root cause of all evils. Tiruvalluvar says "**ava vinmai** 'i.e freedom from desire. Desire for what? Women and wealth. This has been agreed by all saints and even by Lord Krishna. In Geetha he says to Arjuna it is difficult to control the senses, it is to be done by gradual practice of control of senses and renunciation of desire. Tiruvalluvar says "**patruka patratran patrinai appatrai patru vidarku**" (kural, 350). That is, "Desire the desire of Him (i.e. God) who is without desire. This is the only way to eliminate desire".

**Does Desire end if so when?** अङ्गं गलितं पलितं मुण्डं दशनविहीनं जातं तुण्डम्, वृद्धो याति गृहीत्वा दण्डं तदपि मुञ्चत्याशापिण्डम् (angam galitham palitham mundam, dasanaviheenam jaatham tundam, vriddhoyaathi gruhitva dhandam thadhapina muchyat aasapindam) .Your organs may be deteriorated, head has become totally bald, tooth are lost, became infirm and cannot walk without the help of a walking stick; even at this stage the desire remains. Such is the power of desire. Shankaracharya emphasises further. सुखतः क्रियते रामाभोगः पश्चाद्धन्त शरीरे रोगः यद्यपि लोके मरणं तदपि न मुञ्चति पापाचरणम् **(Sukhathahakriyathe raama bhigaha paschaddantha shareere rogaha, yadyapi loke maranam sharanam, thadapi na munchthi paapacharanam).** Even when afflicted by diseases and death is going to be certain, one does not shun form lust. "दिनयामिन्यौ सायं प्रातः शिशिरवसन्तौ पुनरायातः कालः क्रीडति गच्छत्यायु -

स्तदपि न मुञ्चत्याशावायुः (Dinayaminyau saayam praathaha shishirvasanthau pumarayaathaha, kaalaha kreedathi gachchti aayvu thathapina- munchathi aasha vaayuhu). Time moves fast and our days are getting numbered, even then the desire hold us. "अग्रे वह्निः भानुः रात्रौ चुकुकसमर्पितजानुः करतलभिक्षस्तरुतलवास-स्तदपि न मुञ्चत्याशापाशः" **(Agne vahnihi pushte bhaanuhu raathrau chubukasamarpitajaa-nuhu karathala bhikshastharuthalavaasaha thadhapi na munchyat aasapaasaha).** Even after becoming an ascetic, living by begging and sleeping on the roads, even at this stage the desire persists. **Such is the power of Desire.**

For overcoming the attraction towards women Adi Shankaracharya says "नारीस्तनभरनाभीदेशं दृष्ट्वा मा गा मोहावेशम् एतन्मांसवसादिविकारं मनसि विचिन्तय वारं वारम् **(Naari sthana bhara naabhidesam drushtva ma ga mohavesam ethanmaamsa vasaadi vikaaram manasi vinchithaya vaaram vaaram)** . Keep thinking that womens parts are nothing but a modification of fat and flesh. Raja Bhartruhari in vairagya shatakam (वैराग्य शतकम, one hundred verses on renunciation) says a womens face is a seat of phlegm, breasts are lumps of flesh and that one is just excretory system. So it is such type of thinking that brings some renunciation. Whether every one can attain attitude of renunciation like raja bharthruhari after enjoying a lot? His sringara sathakam (श्रृंगार शतकम — reveals how much he has enjoyed women). Ultimately he reached वैराग्य (vairagya) renunciation.

Another obstacle in concentrating on God is wealth. "मूढ जहीहि धनागमतृष्णां कुरु सदबुद्धिं मनसि वितृष्णाम, यल्लभसे निजकर्मोपात्तं वित्तं तेन विनोदय चित्तम". **(Moodha jahihi dhanagama trishna kuru sadbyddhihi manasi vithrushnaam yallabhase nijakarmopaattham vittham thena vinodaya chittam).** Give up the greed .It is foolish to be after amassing wealth. With whatever wealth you get by rightful means, enjoy with that. It is true that wealth is required but amassing wealth following every means is condemned. **Thiruvalluvar said, Kural verse 247- "arul illarku avvulagam illai; porul illarku ivvulagam illagi yangu" (This kural is also recited as "arul illada avvulagam illai; porul illada ivvulagam illai) Though he told about the necessity of wealth in this world thiruvalluvar also says, verse 657 "palimalain they diya aakkathin chanror, kalinal kurave thalai" That is it is better to live in poverty rather than to amass wealth by doing all sins.**

Now a days it is difficult to convince on the above points. We hear of scams of thousands of crores and lakhs of crores, Every sector is commercialised. Unfortunatley education sector as well. Money has become the topmost agenda. Still philosophers may turn out to be right. What is happening now a days will lead to disaster one day or another. **For India, ancient philosophy of simple living and high thinking" is still valid. Another philosopher told "An indian should work like a stallion and live like a saint, if India has to survive".**

"अर्थमनर्थं भावय नित्यं नास्तिततः सुखलेशः सत्यम, पुत्रादपि धनभाजां भीतिः सर्वत्रैषा विहिता रीतिः **(Ardhamanardham bhavaya nithyam naasthi thathaha sukhaleshaha sathyam, puthraadapi dhanabhanjaam bheethi hi sarvatraisha vihitha reethihi;** अर्थमनर्थं भावय नित्यं नास्तिततः सुखलेशः सत्यम्, पुत्रादपि धनभाजां भीतिः सर्वत्रैषा विहिता रीतिः). Wealth is definitely calamitous in- the end. A wealthy man is afraid of his own kith and kin.

Knowing this seek the Lord Govinda (Vishnu).

Now-a-days modern economists are realising the importance of difference between wealth and welfare, peace and prosperity. What we want is peace and welfare.

Understand the power of time and fate and hence don't be arrogant about your bubbling youth, wealth and the people around you. All these would vanish in a minute if time strikes you.

Premature deaths of people with wealth and power are known. Power and wealth and people are fleeting. Hence strive for God/Brahman realisation. Be humble. As **Thiruvalluvar says 'Ellarkum nanram panidal" (verse 125) "nalam vendin nanudamai vendum" (verse 960) .** He who desires good name must desire modesty. So practice humility.

**Why to get salvation?** "पुनरपि जननं पुनरपि मरणं पुनरपि जननीजठरे शयनम्। इह संसारे बहुदुस्तारे कृपयाऽपारे पाहि मुरारे" (punarapi jananam punarapi maranam punarapi janani jathare sayanam, iha samsaare bahudusthaare krupayaa pare paahi muraare) . If you don't attain salvation you will be entering the cycle of births and deaths.. This needs to be avoided. Repeatedly coming back into this world is very painful. As Adi Shankaracharya says in his **"Lakshminrisimha karavalamba sthothram"** – "संसारकूपमतिघोरमगाधमूलं सम्प्राप्य दु:खशतसर्पसमाकुलस्य। दीनस्य देव कृपया पदमागतस्य लक्ष्मीनृसिंह मम देहि करावलम्बम्" **"Samsara Koopam Adhi Ghora Magadha Moolam, Samprapya Dukha Satha Sarpa Samakulasya, Dheenasya Deva Krupana Padamagadasya, Lakshmi Nrsimha Mama Dehi Karavalambam"** This world is very painful. How painful it is? Painful as if hundred serpents are simultaneously biting. Hence one should never come back into this world. That is why one should attain salvation.

**How to get salvation?** "सत्सङ्गत्वे निस्सङ्गत्वं निस्सङ्गत्वे निर्मोहत्वम, निर्मोहत्वे निश्चलतत्त्वं निश्चलतत्त्वे जीवन्मुक्ति: (satssangatve nissangatvam nisangatve nirmohatvam, nirmohatve nischala chittam, nischala chittame jeevan mukthihi) When you are in a good company you will develop non-attachment, which leads to absence of infatuation, which in turn leads to a stable mind and a stable mind leads to liberation. This is the easiest way to attain salvation. Therefore have a good company. "गेयं गीतानामसहस्रं ध्येयं श्रीपतिरूपमजस्रम, नेयं सज्जनसङ्गे चित्त देयं दीनजनाय च वित्तम् (geyam geetha naamasahasram, dhyeyam sreepathi roopa majasram neyam sajjana sange chittam, deyam deena janaaya cha vittham). Reciting Vishnusahsra naamam (thousand names of Lord Vishnu), praying Lord Vishnu, thinking of good people, and distributing wealth among the needy. This is another way of attaining salvation.

**Peace Peace Peace (Om Shanti Om Shanti Om Shanti)**

## G. Names of Allah in Siva Sahasra Naamam (1008 Names of Lord Shiva)

The way Hinduism has sahasranamam's (1008names), Ashtothara satham (108 names) chalisa's (40 verses) trisathi (300 names) etc. Islam has 99 names. of Allah (www.dawateislami.net/gen- eral/devotions/99names). However the way Hindus keep reciting both in the house and priests reciting in temples, reciting the names of the Gods/goddesses in their respective holy places as a formal way of worship is apparently not there in other religions.

What struck me when I have gone through the 99 names of Allah is, some names are similar to what is mentioned in Shiva Sahasranamams. Here is a small list of those. Maybe the equivalents for all the Allah's names in Hindu's compositions cumulatively, one may find... However, all the 99 attributes are totally acceptable to all religions.

1. Al-Khaliq/Al-bari/Al-Mubdi——The creator-Om Dhathraya Namah (ॐ धात्राया नमः)
2. Ar-razzaq/Al-hafiz/Al-Muquit--Sustainer/Protector-Om Dharaya Namah (ॐ धारय नमः)
3. Al-Mumeet- One who reduces the living dead. Bringer of death—Om Sarva Bhootha haraya namah;

Om haraya namah. (ॐ सर्व भूता हराया नमः; ॐ हराया नमः)

4. Ar-Rahman, /Ar- Rahim/Al-Latif--Merciful, compassionate, kind.--Om prasadaya namah; Om bahupradaya namah (ॐ प्रसादाय नमः; ॐ बहुप्रदाय नमः)
5. Al-Aziz/Al-Qahhar /Al-Azim/Al-Qaurec/AlQadir (omnipotent) — Mighty, Power etc.—Om Mahbalaya namaha, Om Balaya Namaha, Om baliney Namaha, Om bala veeraaya namaha (ॐ महाबलाय नमः; ॐ बलाय नमः; ॐ बलिने नमः; ॐ बलवीराय नमः).
6. Al -Alim- Omniscient—Om sarvajnaya Namah (ॐ सर्वग्नाया नमः).
7. Al-Wari- Omnipresent—Om vibhave Namah (ॐ विभवे नमः)

**Peace Peace Peace (Om Shanti Om Shanti Om Shanti)**

## H. Philosophy -A General Discourse

Long time back a great philosopher said "It is the philosophers who should rule the kingdom. Whether philosophers rule the kingdom or not, at least those who rule should know/ have some philosophy. Suppose they don't have?. Under such situation what should we do? It is we people who should have some philosophy. What philosophy we should have?

Dr S. Radhakrishnan said "religion should be cured of their provincialism and must be made to reveal their universality." One should be able to understand the universality among the various religious statements. For e.g. If one says Allah ho Akbar, it is not an Islamic prayer but an universal prayer. It only means God is great. It is so in every religion. Similarly if one says; for thine is the kingdom, the power and the glory forever and ever.; it is not a Christian prayer but applicable to all religions. Like this there are so many statements in every religion which reveal the universality. Remember the great saying "let noble thoughts come to us from every side" (आ नो भद्राः क्रतवो यन्तु विश्वतः, "Aano bhadra krtavo yantu vishwatah").

Let it be any source of religion or faith etc. what is said should have universal application. We should have a catholic view.

Swami Vivekananda acknowledged the superiority of the religions in different aspects. He said "Let us combine the merciful heart of Buddhism, philanthropic attitude of Christianity, brother hood of Islam and spirituality of Hinduism." What is spirituality is difficult to understand as compared to other attributes.

When we talk about philosophy we should not think we are moving away from the world. In fact many books by western authors, on personality development, stress management, success formula books etc the power of prayer, the power of faith and many ideas found in religious scriptures are mentioned. The religious philosophy of simple living and high thinking and harmonious living is also reflected in Lester Brown's book "A new set of values-solutions for the developing countries". (World Watch Institute Washington).

(a) WHO (World Health Organisation) says "My health is at the mercy of those who provokes me. Thus **Anger** which has been repeatedly emphasised in philosophy as an evil is said so also by Doctors.. Another philosopher told "When angry count ten". If the intensity of the anger is more, then count hundred. Another philosopher told that Anger is momentary insanity. In post offices in olden days they used to write "Ek Pal ka Krodh Aap ka Bhavishy Bigaad saktha hai" (एक पल का क्रोध आपका भविष्य बिगाड़

सकता है"). That means a moment of anger can destroy your whole future. Bhagawath Geetha, 2:63- क्रोधाद्भवति सम्मोहः सम्मोहात्स्मृतिविभ्रमः। स्मृतिभ्रंशाद् बुद्धिनाशो बुद्धिनाशात्प्रणश्यति (krodhaadbhavati sammohaha sammohaat smriti vibhramaha. smriti bhramshaad buddhinaasho buddhinaashat pranashyati). Anger leads to confusion, confusion leads to loss of memory and loss of memory leads to loss of reason and intellect and because of this the person is ruined. Hence in the next sloka 2.64, it is advised that a person should control his senses and be free from attachment and aversion as both can lead to anger.

(b) What type of **attitude** we should have?

Bible (New Testament) says, if GOD be for us who can be against us? (Romans 8:31) for what will it profit a man if he gains the whole world and loses his own soul? (Mark 8:36). Geetha says 12:13 (अद्वेष्टा सर्वभूतानां मैत्रः करुण एव च। निर्ममो निरहङ्कारः समदुःखसुखः क्षमी—adveshta sarva bhutaanam maitrah karuna eva cha nirmamo nirahankaaraha. samadukha sukha kshami). One should be friendly and compassionate to everyone, egoless and even minded in pleasure and pain and always forgiving. Other slokas in 12th chapter also emphasise these attitudes. Bible says HE maketh his sun rise on the evil & the good and sendeth rain on just and unjust. Geetha says, be equal to friends and foes.

(c) **God is with form (साकार) or without form (निराकार)?** Hinduism is often criticised for idol worship. Geetha says 12:5 क्लेशोऽधिकतरस्तेषामव्यक्तासक्तचेतसाम् अव्यक्ता हि गतिर्दुःखं देहवद्भिरवाप्यते kleso adhiktaras tesham avyaktha saktha chetasaam, avyaktha hi gathir dukham dehavadbhir avapyate'. That is, it is difficult to concentrate on formless for ordinary beings who are very much attached to the body and the world. Hence start with concentrating on forms and gradually and ultimately reach the formless.

(d) **How can we escape the fear of death**? Think as follows. As Bible says, 'All vanish.—only the city of GOD remains". Why should we fear. If that is so? Jalaludin Rumi says "All except God perishes". By dying I don't become less. I may become angel and then God. Geetha says 2.28, अव्यक्तादीनि भूतानि व्यक्तमध्यानि भारत अव्यक्तनिधनान्येव तत्र का परिदेवना Avyaktha dheeni bhuthani vyaktha madhyaani bhaaratha, avyaktha nidhanaanyeva tatraka paridevana". You were not there at some point of time and you will not be there again at some pint of time in future? Hence why worry? More over what is dead is the body and not the soul which is imperishable 2:20, &2:23. Jewish Talmud says "Body is the sheath of the soul." Body may perish but soul remains ."

A hymn in Bhajagovindam composition gives a solution to escape death/ fear of death. "Bhagawath geetha kinchitha dhheetha gangajalalava kanika peetha sakrudhapiyena muraari samrcha kriyathe tasya yamenana charcha" (भगवद्गीता किञ्चिदधीता गङ्गाजललवकणिका पीता, सकृदपि येन मुरारिसमर्चा क्रियते तस्य यमेन न चर्चा). A little study of Bhagavath geetha, sipping a little water from Ganga river, worship of Lord Vishnu will protect you from the lord of death, i.e. Yama (यम).

(e) **Ultimate purpose** - What is the ultimate purpose of a human being? Sukha praapthi (सुख को पाना) Dukha nivrutti (दु:ख से परे) i.e. getting happiness and getting rid of sorrow. For that what should we do? A story revolving around sage Narada is as follows. Narada happened to master all the 64 branches of knowledge. When he told this to another realised soul, he happened to say "What is the use of mastering these knowledge"? Do they help you from escaping from misery? What is learnt is just branded as inferior knowledge or "Apara vidya". Narada was told to master that by which everything else can be mastered; Attain that by which everything else can be attained; achieve that by which everything else is achieved,; realise that by which everything else can be realised; learn that by which everything else can be learnt. This is called superior knowledge or "para vidya (परा विद्या)".

As to what is this para vidya is difficult to understand and practice. Yet an effort must be made. But the problem is different philosophers may say it differently. We should see what suits us. It does not make any difference which name you utter and which practice you follow. Conviction, devotion, sincerity and perseverance are required. The famous Greek philosophy saying "Know thy Self" is the ultimate purpose of human being. Who are you/Who am I? God or Self or in search of God?. **So think and choose the path.**

**Peace Peace Peace (Om Shanti Om Shanti Om Shanti)**

## I. Universal Ashtotthara Naama satham (108 attributes in Sanskrit) which may

I. Universal Ashtotthara Namma satham (108 Names / Attributes in Sanskrit) which be chanted for any God. (The names do not any way refer to a specific God/Deity, though a few names may seem to indicate so. They have a different meaning. Hinduism has the phenomenon of deification and so has numerous deities. Over a period of time more and more hymns and praises are composed referring to different deities. Whichever deity one praises one does so conferring all the attributes possible supreme. As it is difficult to remember separately compositions/praises of so many deities, here a list is combined which can be used to worship/ praise any deity. Hence memorising just the following 108 names can serve the purpose of worshipping the numerous deities. In future also the practice of composing a set of 108 or any other number of names for some deity or other is very likely to continue. In this endeavour one can pick up names form the following list. Further in practice the praises are made both by reciting individual names and also as a complete string of the names i.e. as sthothram. Some names are mentioned in the list to facilitate that.).

1. Aadhi madhyantha rahithaya namaha-One who is devoid of beginning, middle and end.
2. Aishwaryaya namaha—One who bestows wealth & prosperity.
3. Aartha rakshakaya namaha— One who protects the helpless.
4. Viswa roopaya namaha— One who is of the cosmic form.
5. Janma mrutyu jara vyadhi varjitayanamaha- one who has no birth, death disease and old age.
6. Soukhya pradaya namaha.— One who bestows happiness.
7. Muktidaya namaha—One who bestows salvation.
8. Grahadhi pathaye namaha— one who is the ruler of all planets.
9. Sarvakashta nivarakaya namaha— One who removes all your difficulties.
10. Sarvabhishta phala pradaya namaha.— One who fulfils all your desires.
11. Nityananda phala pradhaya namaha.— One who bestows perennial happiness.
12. Vishnave namaha- All pervading (Here it is not direct addressing of Lord Vishnu by name but as general attribute).
13 Viswam namaha— One who comprises this entire universe.
14. Bhuta bhavya bhavat prabhuh— Lord of the past, future and present.
15. Putatmaya namaha— One whose nature is pure.
16. Paramatmaya namaha— the supreme being.

17. Avyayah namaha— One who who never decays. Immutable.
18. Shivaya namaha— the auspicious one (here it does not mean Lord shiva).
19. Sthanave namaha— One who is firm and changeless.
20. Swayambhuve namaha—One who is self born. He is not begotten.
21. Dhathraya Namaha— the creator
22. Dharaya Namah— the protector
23. Sarva Bhootha haraya namaha— One who can eliminate all living beings.
24. Maha Balaya namaha.— the Mighty
25. Sarvajnaya namaha— Omniscient.
26. Vibhave namaha— Omnipresent
27. Vidhathaya namaha— One who decides the destiny of human beings.
28. Aprameyaha namaha— One who cannot be understood.
29. Sasvataya namaha— One who exists at all times.
30. Pratardanahe namaha—One who destroys ever thing at the time of cosmic dissolution.
31. Jeshtaya namaha— There is nothing that existed before the Almighty
32. Prajapataye namaha— The lord of all living beings.
33. Pragnaya namaha— One who is of the nature of consciousness.
34. Sarveswaraya namaha— The supreme Lord.
35. Achyuthaya namaha— One who never loses his inherent powers.
36. Ameyatama namaha— One whose nature and form cannot be determined.

37. Babruhe namaha— One who governs the world.
38. Viswayoniye namaha— One who is the cause of the world.
39. Lokadhyakshaya namaha— One who is a witness to the whole universe.
40. Anaghaya namaha— One who is sinless.
41. Atindriyaya namaha— One who is beyond our senses.
42. Mahasakthaye namaha— One who is the most powerful.
43. Sthiraya namaha— One who is most stable and is ever of the same nature.
44. Gurave namaha— One who is the teacher of all knowledge.
45. Satyaya namaha— One who is the truth.
46. Dharani dharaya namaha— One who sustains the world with all its components.
47. Visishtaya namaha— One who excels in everything.
48. Naika rupaya namaha— One who is without any form.
49. Ausadham namaha— One who is a curer of all diseases.
50. Satya Dharma parakramah— One who is the truth, virtue & powerful.
51. Prabhave namaha— One who is unparalleled.
52. Ishtaha— One who is liked by all.
53. Dhuryaya namaha— One who takes the burden of all at all times.
54. Brihad bhanave namaha— One who illumines the whole world.
55. Anukulaha— One who is favourable or accessible to all.

56. Viksharaha— One who is without destruction.
57. Gahanah— One who cannot be known by any body.
58. Dharma vidutthamah— One who knows all virtues.
59. Kalaya namaha— One who is the time.
60. Beejamavyayam— One who is the unchanging cause of everything.
61. Sarva darshi— One who is able to see every thing
62. Uttarah— One who is supreme
63. Anantatma— One who is beyond time, space and causation.
64. Gatisattamaha— One who is the ultimate.
65. Bhesajam— One who is the remedy for all evils of this world.
66. Mahabhutaha— One who is beyond past, present and future.
67. Mahan— One who is great.
68. Katitah— One who is the highest.
69. Ayamah— One who is indestructible.
70. Satya Dharma Parayanah— One who is truthful & righteous.
71. Sarvasmai namaha— One who is every thing, all inclusive.
72. Loka palaya namaha— One who is the ruler of all worlds.
73. Sarvakarmane namaha— One to whom all activities belong.
74. Aadaye namaha— One who is the foremost.
75. Nidhaye namaha— One who is the source of all treasures.
76. Animishaya namaha— One who is ever watchful and wakeful.

77. Swayam sreshtaya namaha— One who is innately the most superior.
78. Rudraya namaha— One who is praise worthy.
79. Gataye namaha— One who is the Goal of humanity.
80. Atandritaaya namaha— One who is always active.
81. Ajitaya namaha— One who is invincible.
82. Gambhiraya namaha— One who is profound.
83. Haraye namaha— One who is the remover of all evils.
84. Sarva todya parigrahaya namaha— One who is the owner of all creatures.
85. Tridashaya namaha— One who takes care of three states of mans existence viz; birth, maintenance and death.
86. Praskandanaya namaha— One who wipes out every thing at the end.
87. Atulyaaya namaha— One who is incomparable.
88. Sarva dharine namaha— One who is the upholder of all.
89. Atideeptaaya namaha— One who is extremely luminescent.
90. Siddharthaaya namaha— One who is the accomplisher of every thing.
91. Nihantre namaha— One who can destroy all life.
92. Adambhaya namaha— One who cannot be controlled.
93. Loka kartre namaha— One who is the creator of all the worlds.
94. Aksharaya namaha— One who is imperishable.
95. Prasadaya namaha— One who is compassionate.
96. Upakaraya namaha— One who is most helpful.
97. Priyaya namaha— One who is the most dear.

98. Aninditaaya namah— One who is faultless.
99. Mandhathre namaha— One who is the protector of all beings.
100. Sarvesham Praaninam pataye namaha— One who is the lord of all beings.
101. Sate namaha— One who is the only reality.
102. Achintyaya namaha— One who is beyond our minds.
103. Bahu maalaya namaha— One who has myriad manifestations.
104. Seeladharine namaha— One who is the embodiment of all virtues
105. Amrutaya namaha— One who is like the nectar which bestows immortality.
106. Taaaranaya namaha— One who helps you to overcome difficulties.
107. Satkritaya namaha— One who is held in the highest esteem by all.
108. Sat-chit-ananda-anantam— One who is the truth, knowledge, infinite joy and infinite.

**Peace Peace Peace (Om Shanti Om Shanti Om Shanti)**

(J) Buddhism, Jainism and Sikkhism are all Indian born religions and have many elements and vocabulary of Hinduism. Further religions may have big list of beliefs and "do's and dont's". Hence only vital principles which are unique/ uniquely stated to their respective religions are mentioned here. (To know about Abrahamic relgions— Judaism, Christianity and Islam, readers are recommended to read the book "A brief introduction to Holy Quraan for the present day inquisitive, sceptical and argumentative beginners of all social groups and research oriented academicians in the world" 2017, published by Kalpaz Publications, New Delhi)

**(a) Buddhism**

**"Buddha"** is not the name of the founder of Buddhism but it means **"Enlightened one" or "Enlightenment**). Founder's name is "Siddharta Gautama" who after attaining enlightenment under a bodhi tree (also called commonly as peepal (पीपल) or aswattha (अश्वत्थ) tree. Botanical name is "*Ficus relgiosa*") was called as "Buddha". Their main two denominations are Theravada and Mahayana. In addition to Sanskrit their scriptures are available in the language of Paali.

Buddha taught **four Noble truths** Viz; I) Life is marked by sorrow and suffering (Dukka); II. Sorrow or suffering is caused because of desire and attachment; III) Cessation or elimination of Sorrow or suffering permanently is possible; IV) Path or solution for Cessation or elimination of Sorrow or suffering permanently is to follow the **Eight Fold** path as a result of which one becomes Buddha or enlightened or also called attaining Nirvana. Eight fold path is stated as: 1. Right knowledge/ understanding 2. Right thought 3. Right speech 4. Right action. 5. Right livelihood 6. Right effort 7. Right mindfulness 8. Right concentration.

(**Note**—Here the term 'Right " has to be understood as per the teachings and tradition of Buddhism. In the present times people keep debating as to what is right and what is wrong and they affirm that it is subjective).

Three very popular chantings/ recommendations/ mantras are:

बुद्धं शरणं गच्छामि।

Buddham sharanam gacchami

I seek Buddha for refuge

धर्मं शरणं गच्छामि।

Dhammam sharanam gacchami

I seek Dhamma (Dhamma is a Pali word and the equivalent in hindi/Sanskrit is Dharma) for refuge

संघं शरणं गच्छामि।

Sangham sharanam gacchami

I seek Sangha (community/congregation of monks) for refuge.

**Peace Peace Peace (Om Shanti Om Shanti Om Shanti)**

**(b) Jainism**

Many think that Vardhamana Mahavira was the founder of Jainism. Jainism has 24 Thirthankaras (victorious teachers) , the first one being Rishabhanatha and the last one being Mahavira. A lot of time has passed in between. Followers of Jainism are called "Jains" and they broadly fall under two denominations—Digambaras (naked referring to monks) and swetambaras (wearing white cloths referring to monks) . Mahavira's preachings were compiled into many books and are collectively known as "Agami literature". Their scriptures are found in sanskrit and prakrit besides other languages.

Five fundamental principles are: ahimsa (अहिंसा, non-injury); satya (सत्य, to speak truth); asteya (अस्तेय, not stealing); brahmacharya ब्रह्मचर्य, celibacy and chastity); aparigraha (अपरिग्रह, non-attachment or non-possesiveness to material things).

Jainism believes that ultimate truth or reality (nirvana, निर्वाण is complex and has multiple facets and has to be viewed from many angles. This basic doctrine is called anekantavada अनेकान्तवाद, many-sidedness, or "manifoldness"). After attaining the truth he can be called as Jina or Thrithankara.

**Peace Peace Peace (Om Shanti Om Shanti Om Shanti)**

### (c) Sikkhism

Followers of Sikkhism are called Sikhs. "Sikh, meaning a "disciple", or a "learner". Founder or the first Guru is Guru Naanak who was followed by nine more Gurus. Tenth and the last, "Guru Gobind Singh" did not accept any successor but gave the recommendation of following the scripture "Guru Granth Sahib" as a permanent spiritual guide for the followers. A large portion of this scripture is originally written in the Gurmukhi script developed by second Sikh Guru, Guru Angad. Panjabi language is written in this script.

God is referred to as "Ik Onkaar" (इक ओंकार and "waheguru" वाहेगुरु whose attributes are, Nirankaar (निरंकार, without form), Akaal or Akaal Purkh (अकाल, अकाल, पुरख, timeless i.e beyond time and Alakh Niranjan अलख निरंजन, Invisible). Three pillars of the religion are said to be: 1) naam japo/japna (नाम जपो/जपना, repetition of the divine name), 2) Kirat karo किरत करो, work hard), 3) Vand Chhakko or Vand ke chhakna वंड छक्को, वंड के छकना, sharing with others who are in need). Relgion emphasizes five main virtues Viz; Sat (सत/सत्य, truth); Santokh (संतोख, contentment); Daya (दया Kindnes); Nimrata (निम्रता, being humble); Pyaar (प्यार, love). In view of the above Sikhs greet each other by saying Sat Sri (great) Akaal. They affirm and also say in times of victory "Jo Bole So Nihaal, Sat Sri Akaal". It means whoever utters Sat Sri Akaal shall be happy and would remain blessed.

**Peace Peace Peace (Om Shanti Om Shanti Om Shanti)**

# Part - II

# 444 Points to Ponder

(Note—Many issues/points are highly interconnected/ interdisciplinary. They may be justified grouping under any one of the four categories mentioned below. The same issue/ point can be discussed from various angles. In fact to understand and solve any issue one has to view it from different angles.

## A. Economics, History, Sociology and Politics (EHSP)

1. The situation in our country is very much different from many other countries. Many other countries are highly homogeneous with respect to so many parameters. But our country is a tremendous mixture of people and highly heterogeneous with respect to many parameters-religion, language, social divisions, food habits and day to day culture political ideologies etc. So very difficult for things to work out.

2. Two important constitutional reforms that are required in politics are: to fix the minimum age limit of 35 years to contest for MLA or MP, the way it is a mandatory requirement for president of India etc. and to restrict the total tenure of a politician.

3. Rationalists do not believe in astrology. But for professional astrologers it is worth studying the

horoscopes of various political stalwarts who have witnessed big/unexpected successes and failures.

4. It is embarrassing to often listen to the statement of Winston Churchill — "Indians lack diligence and integrity". We should seriously think over it.
5. Caste is meaningless when men are promiscuous. And men had been promiscuous since ages. Their progeny subsequently all of them have acquired specific caste names following a patriarchal or matriarchal system. Presently patriarchal system that is followed. Government laws have further changed the claims. For example, a lady of other caste if married to a man of an SC (Scheduled Caste) category, even she can claim SC reservation in education, jobs etc besides their children as per patriarchal system of inheritance of caste.
6. In general a state govt employee works only for about 180 days in an year! For the remaining period one can avail legitimate holidays. An university faculty may avail much more leave than the above. India is probably the only country which does not have specific number of mandatory working days in an year and mandatory working hours per week to be followed in both letter and spirit.
7. Students may participate in politics but not at the expense of their education. They should acquire knowledge as expected from the curriculum of their education. That should be their first priority. Students and parents are to be accordingly appraised.
8. Wangar mathai, the Black African woman got a Nobel Prize for peace. She has planted millions of trees and motivated others also to do that and other similar activities involving women. No sophisticated scientific techniques involved in such ventures. Even if you do not get a Nobel Prize, working for mother

nature and society definitely is for the welfare of all and the nation.

9. At least more than 31% of Kerala's economy is supposed to be run by money orders/ remittances from outside Kerala. This figure should be known for all other states. Every state should know as to why its people are leaving the state? For greener pastures? Lack of employment or underemployment? Or any other problem being faced by them?. Accordingly steps should be taken.

10. Knowing fully well that it's illegal, parents allow their children— under aged — to go and come back from schools on two wheelers and even drive in the city. Some drive even four wheelers. Leave aside being illegal, is it not risky for their children? Govt of India for sometime has given advertisement regarding these events with the caution to the parents – "don't unnecessarily boost up the confidence and courage of your children to drive vehicles". However the situation has not changed till today. An added risk is they drive while talking on mobiles simultaneously. This practice of driving talking on mobiles is much more common in adults.

11. It is not sufficient to increase the pay. Government (s) should reduce income tax and other taxes, control the increase in prices of goods and services. Then only the benefit of increasing the pay can be realised by salaried class.

12. Even if the whole country or even the whole world knows that someone is a rapist or a murderer or a criminal you find lawyers coming to his defense!

13. Government should introduce some old age pension scheme for the needy. There are some no. But that is only a pittance. Further government pensioners must be totally exempted from income tax.

14. Could USA Govt. find the conspiracy against the murders of not one but two Kennedys? And afterwards no one from Kennedy's family dare to contest.

15. All media have brought out special issues on the occasion of 50th yr of Indian independence, that's about 21 yrs back. One vital statement made during that time was— We are remaining together not because of any love amongst us!. There is no love lost if we break apart. But we are remaining together because it's not— for some reasons— possible to break apart and live separately. For e.g. if broken apart each region has to defend itself maintaining a separate military etc. If that happens, every region will be weak to defend itself against any invaders and region after region it would be easy for them to conquer and the whole nation will be under invaders. An inevitable outcome if our divisive tendencies go to extreme. Hence it's necessary to work for the unity and integrity of the nation. Hope this sense will prevail forever.

16. Compared to the average percentage of overall India, Hindus are found in greater percentage, in 16 states of India with Himachal Pradesh ranking the highest followed by Madhya Pradesh.; Muslims in 6 states of India with J & K ranking the highest followed by Assam & West Bengal and Christians in 9 states of India with Nagaland ranking the highest followed by Mizoram & Meghalaya. Most of the Sikhs are confined only to Punjab. Religion and caste are two important parameters in Indian electoral politics— also called vote bank politics or electoral arithmetic— besides, region, language and political ideology.

17. Sex education in educational institutions is still a taboo in India. Of course Government is spending

money on AIDS awareness. Because of lack of sex education and social stigmas there had been a rise in the number of both legal and illegal abortions and matrimonial problems.

18. What is puzzling & disgusting is, public do not feel a sense of belongingness / ownership towards public/ state properties –in other words their own properties!? Will they destroy their own personal cars, two wheeler's or their personal properties? Why they don't have a similar belongingness towards public properties? Public should be educated as to how to lodge their protests.

19. When there are two variables, there will be 4 combinations. Economic status and merit are two different variables. So you have those who are (a) Economically poor but have merit. (b) Economically poor and don't have merit either. (c) Economically well but don't have merit. (d) Economically well and have merit as well. So only category 'a' and category 'd' must get into educational system with category 'a' requiring economic support. Is it possible to ensure that only -a- and -d- will be able to get into the system? 'c' are able to get into private institutions. And 'c' are also able to get public jobs because of they being economically well off! Category "c" - also must be prevented to get into the public system.

20. In India we are currently facing a peculiar situation. Many big shots taking loans from banks, cumulatively amounting to several lakhs of crores. and not paying back and law is not able to deal with them. In the recent demonetisation, more than 95% of the demonetised currency notes have supposed to have been come back to RBI!! Apparently people were successful in converting almost all of their black money into white. People should think over it.

21. Telugu people (Andhra Pradesh and Telangana) who constitute the single largest majority visiting Sabarimala (Pilgrim place of God Ayyappa in Kerala) from outside Kerala.

22. A politician will do anything to keep up his job. (this sentence itself is complete in sense. No need to add anything.) But the complete quotation is as follows: "A politician will do anything to keep up his job. Even become a patriot". So voters must be vigilant and extremely responsible.

23. It's not possible to be all the time very cautious while speaking. With many in fact we talk casually, informally, jovially without straining our brains. So others should be considerate enough to accommodate errors in communication. They must allow us the freedom to retrieve anything we said— without any conseuquences or offence— which we should not have. Otherwise life would be very serious and loses its charm. Common man should have enough of freedom of speech, carefree talk with his companions or fellow citizens without any repercussions. For a common man socializing and speaking is the only affordable past time.

24. In the recent times there is a lot of hue and cry regarding women not being allowed in ceratin temples. Do women really want a little separate space for their spiritual pursuits? Neither men nor women should bother if any temple (s) is/are exclusively devoted to each of them. Hindu religion has no shortage of temples. They are a huge number and any one can visit any one of them. Gender based temples are countable as compared to the vast number of temples where both men and women can enter. And women visit all these temples. In one temple in kerala, both men and women are allowed but at different times. This is again an exception.

More over there is a paradox in case of the diety Ayyappan. In Ayyappan temples elsewhere in the country both men and women of all ages are allowed unlike in sabarimala (kerala) where only women after menopause are allowed

Creating separate space for males and females is there in other sectors also. For e.g. we have educational institutes separately for males and females and also coeducational. Former are less. Though they can study in the institute exclusively meant for them, many boys and girls prefer to study in co-educational institutions!

25. When Hong Kong was to be surrendered back to Chinese, many Chinese and others in Hong Kong didn't want to live under mainland communist China. Many fled to other countries not as illegal refugees but as legal migrants apparently by depositing in their countries enough money. Hong Kong people knew much in advance when British are going to hand it over to mainland China and so they planned well in advance.

26. A few times there was news in the media saying that highly qualified people are applying for class four posts (for which only tenth class pass is the requirement) . We should also think alternatively. It is not unemployment that is rampant but higher and professional education that is rampant. It is indiscriminate bringing of people into education and poor quality of education. Education expansion must be linked to job opportunities and the situation must be duly appraised to the public. Increasing Gross Enrolment Ration without visualising avenues and revenues for employment is unwise.

27. A Chinese thinker. said —Concentrate on agriculture and industry and try to have a frugal living; the state

will never be impoverished. A country like ours should seriously think on such sayings. Of course there is one lacuna in the above quote—Chinese man has not mentioned the defence requirements for a country which takes a heavy toll. And Chinese know this very well as they have borders with many countries and want to emerging as a force to reckon with.

28. The craze for Government jobs is because of large number of holidays which can be legally availed, less accountability of work turned out by the employee, no fear of retrenchment but can happily continue till retirement age 58 or 60 yrs, post retirement benefits and some medical security (if not in all sectors) and possibility of making money otherwise (if not in all sectors). Naturally there is a cutthroat competition and can involve malpractices in recruitment. The above are also the reasons as to why sometimes many highly qualified candidates apply for much lower posts in government.

29. Long time back, Netherlands government has undertaken a Pre-natal, Post-natal and Child care program, intensively and extensively. As a result the average height of the Dutch people has increased by two inches plus! So it is not sufficient that Government extends maternity leave but also provide for the health care of the women during pregnancy and initial child care.

30. One/media should not hesitate to mention specifically the name of the caste (s) involved and the place where they come from, in any criminal incidence. Why should we use general terms/ broad categories? If you take into consideration divisions and sub-divisions and sub-sub divisions in each of the broad categories in each state of India there will be thousands of

different communities. Let the public and the officials and politicians know who are they and where they belong to.

31. In the recent floods in Chennai (Madras), it was revealed that 16 percent of Tamil nadu lives in Chennai! Similarly a news that Bangalore may have to be evacuated in another ten years due to water scarcity. Similar problems in Bombay too. Ill planned accommodation of people and establishments should not be allowed in any state capital and also in national capital. Decongestion is a must. They should assess how many they should accommodate and what to accommodate. Poor urban planning is a serious problem in the country.

32. Both public and Government are concerned about liquor drinking assuming evil proportions. Many feel that if freebies (distributing various items to the public free of cost) and welfare schemes are withdrawn, drinking is very likely to be reduced. The money which an house hold earns from their work would be utilised for their needs i.e for the items to be purchased which are presently being given free of cost and through welfare schemes. But there is every fear that the government may be defeated in the elections if the present schemes are withdrawn. In fact political parties try to win the election by promising more and more incentives to the voters.

33. Interestingly Bethlehem, the birth place of Jesus Christ has a Muslim majority! Even Israel which Jews have opted to live after the second world war has 16% Muslims. And neighbouring places too have a Muslim majority. Palestine is predominantly Muslim. West bank (85%) Gaaza (99%) Jordan (95%). Lebanon (54%). So among the three Abrahmic religions, Prophet Muhammad's influence

predominated more in these regions. Though the influence of Jesus Christ could spread to distant places it could not spread to the nearby places!

34. Punishment for a crime across the globe has been varying from time to time and country to country. Both in India and across the globe there are people for and against capital punishment. Even among those who are for capital punishment vary in the mode in which they are to be killed. India adopts hanging. In other countries it can be by electric chair or by lethal injection. Similarly for rape some countries want to do or are already doing chemical castration. Some countries sentence him to jail for varying periods of time. Punishment for Marital rape (i.e. sexual involvement with one's own wife without her consent) is an embarrassing legal issue being discussed in India. When Swedish prime Olof Palme was murdered in 1986 the implications of the Swedish law was discussed. The law was, if you can't find the criminal within 10 yrs, you can't punish the criminal even if caught afterwards, whatever may be the offense. What life imprisonment means may be different in different countries. It can be till the end of one's life or only for a particular period of time.

35. India has a peculiar case. Phoolan devi has committed many murders and organized rapes. She got elected and became an MP (member of parliament). True Atrocity was committed on her by others and she became a victim in her past. But does that entitle her to commit the above crimes, get absolved and even get elected to the parliament? As per news paper reports, the number of legislators and parliamentarians with criminal antecedents/ cases pending are very high.

36. Drinking liquor is very common among those who are below 21 among duly educated, less educated and

uneducated A legal point is when an 18 year old has the right to vote, does one not automatically get a right to drink?

37. (a) Man was originally a food hunter and food gatherer. Since he thought of agriculture, dependency on food has easened not only for those who are doing agriculture but also to others and so they could spend time in other pursuits. And civilizations developed.

From that time till now the situation of the farmers was varying from time to time and place to place and from time to time even within the same place.

(b) In olden days there was no so much of population, goods and services from science and technology, consumerism and need to defend countries. Now we have all these to a detrimental level.

(c) We are presently 134 crore plus people, projected to increase at the rate of 1 to 2 percent annually at least till 2030 or even till 2050. So now we should think. How much food is required for all of them? How much land is required to produce the required food? How many are required to provide? Whom do you expect to think on these lines and implement?

38. When there was some controversy about some acquitted persons, a court points out where the faults lie! It says:

(a) "Most of the acquittals are due to the ineptness and inability of the police to perform duty professionally, which is some-times also a result of political interference."

(b) "Drastic improvement in investigation by the police and reduction of political interference is needed".

(c) Poor investigation of the crime by the police.

(d) High court was also critical about their own fraternity at lower levels by saying "they have a faulty appreciation of evidence.

So this is something serious for all to think.

39. Kerala is a little state but with 14 medical colleges. They have not only surpassed the WHO (World Health Organisation) recommendation but are on par and even surpassed many other countries in the ratio of doctors to patients—In Kerala it is 1: 700. No need to say it is nowhere in the country.

40. Apart from the local pressures, international analysis of our country and recommendations are deciding our planning and priorities. They tell/pressurize us regarding how many scientists/doctors etc per unit population we should have, what should be our gross enrollment ratio in education at various levels, and they give a poor impression of our country regarding poverty levels, human development index, etc. So we have to accordingly tailor our planning. They interfere in all our local affairs. We have to respond to that too. Politicians have their own problems. How to win in the elections? So it is people who should seriously ponder and participate in policy planning.

41. Ours is not a country but more aptly an aggregation of so many countries. Every state is like a country. Each of our state is equivalent or even more compared to other countries. Currently we have 29 states and 7 union territories. There is a likely hood of having more states. Each state over a period of time is bound to demand for a separate IIT, IIM, AIIMS, IISER, IIIT, medical/agriculture/veterinary/language/ central university etc. This process may be delayed but unlikely to stop. How about the prospects of man power coming out from so many institutes?

42. Though there has been no third world war, there were many wars after second world war and the number of people killed in these wars are much more than the number of people killed in both the world wars together. Secondly though all the countries were not involved, some countries got into many of the above wars both directly and indirectly.

43. Hooch (spurious/adulterated liquor) tragedies are primarily because of the adulteration with methanol. Though many died or have gone blind, no action was taken on anyone. Owners are so powerful!

44. We have cases where in the same family, different members are affiliated to different political parties! And people do not mind electing them!

45. Collecting Road Toll is increasingly being felt as an exploitation. Toll is there in several places in the country. No one knows how long they will be collecting the money?. How much money they have collected till now and how much more money they will be collecting in the future? What exactly is the deal between the contractor and the respective government? A few may know.. Some big shot should file an.. RTI (Right to Information act) for all existing tolls so that the above information is known to general public.

46. Since olden days over a period of time if observed we find Indians using various products..Made in U.S., UK, Germany, Korea, Taiwan, Japan, Switzerland, China etc. Recently PM Modi has initiated the project of "Make in India"). Even agricultural products we had been importing from several other countries. One point that needs mention is, making in India unnecessary consumer and fancy goods may be stopped as recommended long back by Lester Brown of World watch Institute, Washington, USA. More

than any other products, making in India defence products should be a priority as import of defence weapons from other countries deplete lot of our foreign reserves. We cannot become a power to reckon with always depending on others. We should be self sufficient.

47. British while leaving India predicted balkanisation/ fragmentation of India sooner or later. Though the country has not fragmented, there was fragmentation within the country. Now we have more number of states and more number of districts within a state. And this trend is likely to continue. At country level, Kashmir is still trying to detach from India. Some divisive tendencies were exhibited in some other parts of the country. We have to function, coherently, diligently and intelligently to remain together.

48. Fire Crackers have come very late into our civilization. Now it has become an economic activity and so it will continue though environmentalists, rationalists etc. may keep commenting on it. Recently it has become politics and crime also because of Chinese crackers.

49. If we cannot take care of our old parents how can we expect to take care of cows? Who will incur the expenses and why? It is not only cows even other animals are killed much before their natural life span. Human survival takes priority. Though slaughtering of cattle etc, are allowed at all places for consumption, stray dogs which have become a menace are not allowed to be killed.

50. Though Egypt technically may come under Africa they are not negroes.

51. Problems with neighbouring countries is one of our serious problems.

52. Difference between need, desire, luxury and greed has become difficult nowadays. Good food, reasonable clothing, & shelter, different electronic and non-electronic gadgets at home, money for children's education and family health care. Religious & cultural functions, travel, etc etc. All these are considered as needs of the family. Can they be fulfilled that too for such a huge population/ large number of households?

53. With mind boggling social heterogeneity –thousands of communities — Social conflicts are very likely. One should seriously think about it.

54. As on today after Christians and Muslims, the third largest group in the world is that of atheists plus agnostics and related groups (termed as "Unaffiliated"). Long time back Hindus were there in the third position.

55. It's strange in India there are people asking for ban on liquor but not a ban on tobacco. Tobacco cultivation should be banned and the same land be used to grow some useful food crops to feed the huge population. Further, most of the medical Doctors agree that nearly 75% of the total cancers are due to tobacco and liquor.

56. Someone should analyze the difference in the price which a farmer is getting and the consumer is paying and duly account for the difference and take suitable action accordingly. The difference can be quite high.

57. We can't have as many toilets as the number of the people. If in a household there are 5 to 6 people and all have to finish their toilet at more or less the same time, each house should have 5 to 6 toilets which is impossible. So either they should be in apposition or adjust the timings or have to come out for open defecation. This happens.

58. All the nations concerned along with UNHCR and UN should solve the crises that lead to the flow of immigrants from different parts of the world and put the immigrants back into their respective nations.

59. Hope people will realize the causes, consequences of and solutions for space constraints.

60. Conquering others and inflicting sufferings was there even before deadly weapons were discovered. Earlier we had swords etc and now we have deadly weapons. Weapons are both for defense and offense, if need be. As Shakespeare told revenge is sweet even if it comes late. We don't know who wants to settle scores with whom, if an opportunity comes. Both the fear of being conquered and the urge to conquer is there with many. Hence the need to have arms rather better arms. Acquiring ability to attack from outer space/ planets is thought as an endeavour in view of the above.

61. This is a problem since long. Are we Indians crossing the International borders knowingly or unknowingly? If we are crossing knowingly we deserve whatever the opponent country decides. If we are crossing unknowingly then Indian navy has a serious responsibility to clearly demarcate the borders and duly caution the people. Problem is there on land borders also. Often justification is given saying that we have very long borders and is difficult to guard. Defence ministry should invest its intellect and capital as to how to overcome this problem? Fisherman and / or others had been crossing sea or land borders with Sri Lanka and Pakistan.

62. Livelihood, economic status and social status are more important than environmental status at least for now and the near future. So talking about vehicular or industrial pollution does not carry much

significance and make an impact. Can we strike a balance?

63. Governments are appointing people even to higher posts with doubtful integrity and inefficiency. So the people keep saying always. But how about people? Are they not happily electing candidates as MLA's MP's etc with criminal antecedents or criminal cases pending on them? Once somehow a momentum has gathered and a resolution was to be passed to debar candidates from contesting elections who have criminal antecedents or criminal cases pending on them. Something incredible happened then! All political parties have stopped the resolution! People did not protest!

64. ST's (Scheduled Tribes) are altogether a different lot. Say for example people in some north eastern states. Similarly in other places. Addressing or discussing them combining together with SC's (scheduled castes) or forming joint associations is inappropriate.

65. There can be exceptional situations. When erstwhile USSR collapsed, there was a chaos in east Europe, and the Berlin wall—wall between east and west Germany collapsed. People from east Germany were running in panic towards the wall, cross it and enter into west Germany. During this process many mothers have abandoned their babies and ran towards the wall and crossed into west Germany. The photos of abandoned babies were projected on TV channels. Obviously, many others have abandoned their kith and kin to enter into West Germany. Why they behaved like that?. This makes one philosophical!

66. Do we have politicians who can be condemned in our country?? Whom you call as politicians— good, bad or worse— are regarded by the respective social

groups as their most venerable leaders. So X calls your most venerable leaders as politicians and you call the most venerable leaders of X. as politicians.

67. Agriculture and religion are two vital things in India and so many outsiders try to interfere in both. Unfortunately the situation now is, the status of God men also is determined on the basis of number of western followers the God men enjoys. The way scientists are asked, how many publications you have in international journals, papers presented in international conferences, visits abroad etc, God men also are asked how many international followers you have and how many countries they have visited etc!

68. Man is not contented with living with little food and live an extremely frugal life. He has so many other desires. How can you meet them without population control? Just because agricultural scientists feel that they are capable of feeding 10 billion people, that does not mean you don't bother about population control and allow to grow the population up to 10 billion. That would be otherwise a disaster for different countries. Most of the above rise in population will be only in countries like India etc.USA and other developed western countries, though they had food surpluses and good economic status since long, kept their population in check all through and will continue to do so.

69. The craze of Indians to possess gold is the main cause for the smuggling. As long as there is a heavy demand there will be smuggling. It is said that cumulatively Indian people possess more gold than Govt. of India. (One can add temples to it). Like income tax can government take any steps in putting a ceiling on the amount of gold which an house hold can have? Government is linking aadhaar card with so many

things. Let it be linked to purchases from jewellery shops.

70. Younger generations are forgetting or forgot or indifferent partitioning of India. Events around these time were horrifying. Nation should also stand in silence for 2 minutes on 15th of August.

71. Ancient scriptures like Vedas, Bible etc were preserved by word of mouth, till print was invented. Such was the memory power of some people which was as much required. Preserving the already generated knowledge is a very great contribution by itself. They are as superior. Even today there are people with great memory power. They may not get a Nobel prize but they serve a noble purpose. They are as great, even if they can't think anything new.

72. There is still a feeling in the society that daughter is a liability. And obsession for a male child is still there. If a daughter doesn't return home in time from the school, college, office etc, or daughter working in night shifts, parents are very much worried. Increased crime has added to the tension. Gender ratios are so much in favour of males in some states where the society has a feeling of liability and tension with a daughter to be brought up.

73. It's an old saying that more blood has been shed in the name of religion than any other cause. [Of course it is still taking place].However subsequently much blood has been shed for other reasons. Out of the total 1763 wars only 7% of them were related to religious causes and in these wars only 2% of the total people were killed. So the vast majority of wars and people killed in wars are not related to religious causes. Now coming to a cure for religious wars, Dr S. Radhakrishnan said. "Religions must be cured of

their provinciality and must be made to reveal their universality. Who can do that?

74. According to Swami Vivekananda, education means building up of character and this is not possible in this era. One wants to survive and enjoy at any cost. The "one" I have mentioned can refer to any level of organisation—individual, a social group, a state, a nation, a religion a political party etc. The brain has undergone an incredible transformation. No one wants anyone to interfere in his survival, personal happiness, desires, aspirations ambitions etc, So people are following only what is convenient to them in the religion and the religious scriptures.

75. India is a land of paradoxes. We have— small houses with more family members;. households with small incomes but more family members; more degrees (educational qualifications) but less income.; less number of degrees but more income.

76. There was a shop who used to keep a board....Beware of duplicate products! He himself was selling duplicate products! This is true in many cases. Few examples

    (a) They write...only permitted colors used. In fact not.

    (b) Many local chemical companies supply chemicals with chemical composition and purity as indicated on the pack of International companies or any standard company. In fact their chemicals are of inferior quality.

    (c) Duplicate drugs..They write the same description and concentration of active ingredient etc like those of the standard companies. So even if rules and conditions are imposed they may follow them only in letter and not in fact or in spirit.

77. People are more practical than ideal in settling for a partner. A man may not be truly loving a girl but still settle for her because of other reasons. It may be true with women too! So we do talk of marriages of convenience and there had been many such. Sacrifices and compromises are common in finalizing the marriages both for men and women.

78. The very fact that we have UNHCR (United Nations High Commission for Refugees) reflects the serious of the problem of "refugees". Those who go to other countries legally—irrespective of the nature of jobs they do— are called as "economic Refugees". Within the country we may have inter-state migration and intra-state migration of people because of more than one reason.

79. Kerala might have been successful in avoiding child labour but could not avoid large scale migration of adult labour to Guelph countries and other places. In India even adults are not interested in doing labour. We have to depend on Bangladeshi immigrants and Nepalese. We are more happy to do in other countries or live otherwise.

80. In Andhra Pradesh 34000 acres of land— a large part of this is supposed to be fit for doing agriculture— has been acquired for the construction of the new state capital. Only time has to tell the consequences of this on agricultural production in that particular region and the meeting of local demands for food and the number of farming families who have discontinued farming and the farm labour who were depending on those lands. But according to some the land owners are happy as their annual income is now more than their past income from agriculture as they got remunerative price for their land surrendering. The same logic can apply elsewhere too more

effectively. If farm land can give more price if sold as real estate then farmers may prefer to sell away the land. This price will be definitely much more than what a Government can give /gives. Consequence is, number of farmers and farm land decreases with time but population remains the same or increases. Even otherwise at many places in the country number of farmers who want their sons to continue in farming is considerably decreasing with time. We have to think of ways to ensure food production with lesser and lesser number of farmers and on lesser and lesser land in future.

81. A weak nation saying it is tolerant or being termed as tolerant is meaningless. India had been, is and will probably continue to be a weak nation. It should become a superpower to reckon with to have any say in the international scenario.

82. Ambedkar would not have opted for Buddhism unless he has made it doubly sure that Buddhism is free from and would be free from the custodians of Hinduism. A second reason could be that many other countries are also influenced by Buddha and Buddhism who can be helpful. Though Ambedkar has opted for Buddhism, other SC's (scheduled Castes) in India are very diverse and found in other religions.

83. If there is no single party majority, there should be re-election. That makes the people more responsible. Running coalition governments is not desirable. Secondly for a candidate, there should be a certain percentage of total votes fixed. Only when a candidate gets this fixed percentage of votes the candidate should be declared as won. Presently in multi-cornered contests, the winning candidates votes are less in number compared to the total number of votes polled –cumulatively—to the candidates who have lost the election; in other words votes polled against

the winning candidate are more. Many say a candidate should get at least 50% plus of the total votes in the constituency to be declared as won. Then voters would be responsible and their turn out also would be more.

84. In the developed west where social, economical, academic and intellectual freedom are high, total unfoldment of one's personality-which should be one's aim— is possible.

85. In the developed west personal life and professional life are separate and don't get mixed up.

86. There is a lot of controversy in one of the Indian science congress about discussing Hindu science in vedic era & mythology. One session was devoted to that. It is a paradox. On one side people say to validate our ancient scientific wisdom and on other side they object to discuss about that for a short time in a congress/conference?. Not only in Hindu civilisation, many other civilisations also have mythology, practicing of traditional medicine, knowledge of various arts and branches of knowledge, had diversity of infrastructure, weapons etc. Hence all civilisations need to know their past wisdom.

87. Eleven percent of worlds gold is supposed to be hidden with Indian families! .We constitute 18 % of the world's population. Of the imported Gold nearly 24% is supposed to be only with one state—Andhra Pradesh (now state is divided in to Andhra Pradesh and Telangana).

88. If people see only similarities and live together, there is no problem. Most of the problems in the country/ world are because of people looking the differences among them. So see commonalities and also try to know how to cope up /adjust with the differences among the various groups of people.

89. Among all the groups in the world, negroes were exploited the most. Maximum atrocities were perpetrated on them not just by one group but every group which had an opportunity. And even today they are in a bad shape with no hope of future. In fact James Watson— Co-discoverer of DNA double helix and Nobel Prize winner— expressed the opinion that they have no hope after visiting their countries! UN should intervene.

90. Iran Govt. should be praised for giving so much freedom for women to pursue higher education. (In connection with an Iranian woman getting the highest award -Fields Medal in Mathematics which is equivalent to Nobel Prize).

91. Decent salary, proper machinery and gadgets and medical security should be given to all these people who are prone to occupational hazards.

92. Best option which government should enforce by law is "electric chair" for the disposal of the dead. It is economical, environmental friendly, less time and space consuming.

93. More than any party it's the people who may have to be blamed because of the following: (a) Heavy boozing (b) Drug abuses (c) Heavy migration to other countries and from one state to another, leaving their families behind. (d) living beyond means.

94. Politicians/Political parties are supposed to have 4 M's to survive. Money power, Muscle power, Man power and Media power.

95. Governments talk aobut "smart cities". First priority should be to convert existing metros/ state capitals into smart cities. Decongest them. Depollute them. And prevent further dumping of men and matter and establishments in the same metros / capitals. These

points are to be kept in mind while trying to convert any other place into a smart city.

96. Nip the evil in the bud. Let governments ban the manufacturing of the mentioned plastic items. Ban their licenses. Anyone still found to do so take legal action on them. Public will automatically adjust to the absence of plastic items.

97. CAPART— council for advancement of people's action and rural technology— has made a survey and declared that most of the NGO's (Non-Governmental Organisations) are bogus. No action was taken. Rather they have further increased.

98. If you violate the rules and regulations, that means you do not know administration! Because there is nothing which one cannot do or undo within the frame work of rules and regulations. Our administrative set up is such.

99. It may be true that "patriarchal setup" is dominating. But the father, brother and other menfolk related to the women are also males. Why they want their daughters and sisters and kith kin to .suffer in any way!?

100. There is a fundamental difference when Muslims say – 'no to dowry" and Hindus saying - "no to dowry". Muslims say so because dowry is against Islam religion. Rather the boy has to pay Mahr (bridal money) to the girl. This the boy has to do as it is prescribed in Islam. Hindus making hue and cry about dowry is not because religion prohibits it. But it has assumed evil proportions.

101. There are so many parameters on which one can be discriminated- language, caste, region, religion, political affiliation etc. It's inevitable in India.

102. Many feel it's wrong—in any case inappropriate — to take oath on Bhagwath Githa in courts. We should

take oath on Vedas, which are the primary authorities of Hindus. Belief in Vedas is one of the basic tenets of Hinduism and they were existing long before Bhagwath Githa.

103. Money is with whom? Recent news item is "In 2017, around 73 percent of India's wealth belonged to 1 percent of its 130 crore plus people (current population is 134 crore plus). It increased from 58 percent a year ago, indicating that economic inequality has widened in 2017. In other words it means only 27% of wealth is with the remaining 99% of the population. How to categorise the remaining 99%? One common way is to classify as, middle class, poor, and BPL (below Poverty Line) . Some economists have further divided the middle class into three categories Viz; Upper middle class; Middle class and Lower middle class. Methodology, definitions and benchmarks for categorising people as above have been varying. Hence there is a need to seriously debate and categorise the population accurately as per economic status. (Personally I do not mind anyone having hundreds or thousands or lakhs of crores. What I want is a decent living for myself. And that is /should be the aspiration of the people. And it is towards this goal the government and people should work).

104. British have ruled all the countries in the world whose names start from A to Z, except 'X'. It appears that there were no countries in the world whose names start with X! Starting with 'X" there is no country even today.

105. It's not an issue of Muslim, Hindu, Christian etc nor OC, OBC, SC, etc. It's to be reflected on a different plane. It's the problem of gender— males versus females. Since Nature/ God has created males

physically stronger than females with the added problems of menses, pregnancy & baby care. Males in all the above categories exploit women in different ways. What is to be discussed and assured is safety, security, lively hood, freedom and no social stigmas for anything to the females.

106. Highest infertility among Paarsis (their religion is Zoroastrianism). Their population has dwindled to about 60 thousand.

107. Simply impossible to please all the 134 crore plus people of our country. So the next best, is a concept called "utilitarian ethics"; that is maximum good to maximum number of people. So the Government should try to bring laws based on the above concept.

108. In these modern days even husband and wife remain separated (without any intention of divorce) as they do jobs in different places and meet occasionally. Only after retirement they live together.

109. India which has a huge population, one should not insist on talking only in terms of percentages. One should also talk rather only talk in terms of absolute numbers. For e.g. we have more number of educated people than the total population of USA, more number of internet users and mobiles etc.

110. One should know that in our country there are many parents who say—we don't mind living alone or in old age homes but our children must be in USA, Canada, Europe etc. So it is not daughter in laws—as often criticised — but it is the parents own making to live in separation. Statistics confirm this. Number of geriatrics (old people) living alone and the number of old age homes have increased in India.

111. German Hahnemann's homeopathy and German Chiero's numerology and palmistry is more followed

and respected in India than in any other country including Germany!

112. A recent survey –in some pockets of India —says 40 to 50 percent of children have said that it is the parental pressures that decides their career, jobs and even marriage!

113. No doubt. Ancient Greeks were so great. They had so many great philosophers and rich philosophy. Yet they have become a different affiliation now!

114. Many professionals—engineers, doctors, teachers in colleges and universities etc. joined / want to join IAS and allied services and also State Public Service Commissions.

115. Tamil nadu in particular, cinefield and politics seem to be intertwined. To enter into politics you have to come through cinefield!. Erstwhile Andhra Pradesh followed Tamil Nadu to some extent. Outside south—Bollywood also has number of examples. Kerala people never seems to be carried away and elected anyone from the cine field. To become a Doctor or an engineer etc you require a formal qualification in the respective subject. To join politics one does not require any formal qualification. Can we insist?

116. Not all states follow the fixed upper limit of 50% communal reservation. It can exceed. States are asking to reveal the recent census data clearly at the earliest to facilitate their demand to increase the reservation percentage. Many states are sure that as per the recent census reserved category can be anywhere from 60 to 75%. Religious Minorities are yet to demand reservation. Many still confuse. Be clear. Unreserved category, designated as GT, means General turn—i.e anyone can apply and get appointed. It's not exclusively meant for those who don't fall under reserved category.

117. Urdu is not a language of Muslims in the world. Urdu is a language of Muslims in the Indian subcontinent only (however they had their own languages in addition to Urdu) . In India depending on the region Muslims may know urdu or may not urdu. The real language of Muslims is to be identified with Arabic as Quran is in Arabic. Next comes Persian and Turkish. In fact Persian was the court language during the rule of many Mughals in India.

118. Our constitution is either paradoxical or has relics of the past. When in the highest court the judge pronounces death penalty for some one, president can condone it! But it is not treated as contempt of court!

119. Male child obsession sometimes takes a different form— for the sake of a male child, the parents keep on producing 4, 5 or even 6 girl children! A few don't succeed in producing a male child even after that! One of the reasons for population explosion.

120. Imagine the time taken for a case to reach up to the supreme court! Not only undue delay, even judgment can be totally different between lower courts and supreme court! How is that judges differ so much? Imagine two doctors giving altogether different treatments to the same type of patients! Out of court settlements probably can ensure speedy justice. But not going to court is inevitable in many cases. Crime is there and crime rate has increased a lot in all social strata.

121. The question of export comes/ should come only when there is a surplus. Do we really have anything surplus? People's purchasing capacity is apparently very low. With 134 crore plus population can we have anything in surplus? Only population we have in surplus and that can be exported!

122. Many are of the opinion that majority of the Kashmiris want to be with Pakistan. In olden days also plebiscite was not conducted as initially promised by some leader, only for this very reason. Pakistan attacking Bangladesh is well known. Because Muslims in Pakistan do not identify themselves with Bengalis and Vice Versa. That is why Kashmiris often speak of both the Kashmir regions—of India and Pakistan—come together and remain as a separate nation. Very likely their real ambition is that.

123. Events can take any turn. When Pakistan invaded Bangladesh did India not physically entered and fought? India entered Srilanka also. Same thing happened in Vietnam when US & Chinese forces have entered. And in Afghanistan where both US and USSR entered. Did anyone forecasted such a turn of events? And the outcome was different in the above situations. US, USSR etc and UN peace keeping forces entered many countries. Even USA and USSR had to withdraw/ withdrawn without solving the problems of the nations they entered. And India is not such a big power to reckon with compared to USA, USSR etc. Is it not the duty of exclusively UN Peace Keeping Forces in the above situations?

124. Nothing to worry about US or for that matter the developed west even. It is not that every body in the developed west is great. But they always had, have and continue to have a significant number of people with exceptional calibre and commitment who can contribute and take care of the nation. Unfortunately India is inadequate in this requirement.

125. Long back a senior politician has admitted that corruption is a reality. He said. Bureaucratic corruption is rooted in political corruption and

political corruption is rooted in electoral corruption. So whom to blame for corruption? Think!

126. Even today a large number of negroes in African countries remain severely undernourished and suffer from starvation. Rich Christian and Muslim nations. who have got the negroes converted into their respective religions have a moral responsibility to uplift them.

127. Eugenics was practiced all over the world even today.

128. Unfortunately we had been listening to honour killings where men and women form different social strata have got married or want to marry. Such marriage shave been taking place in Indian civilisation since ages.

129. Is it right voters don't require any educational qualifications to vote? Leaving aside educational qualifications the age factor is a vital one. Initially minimum age limit to vote was 21 years. But subsequently it was reduced to 18 years. At this age definitely the person's maturity and independence is not enough to vote. It is better we revert back to 21 years limit. Let us not compare ourselves with some other countries who are following 18 years limit. For our country's state of affairs 21 years makes more sense.

130. In India the situation is like this, in all sectors. As long as there is a giver (one who gives the bribe), there is a taker (one who takes the bribe). And there are many givers.

131. India's GDP is 1, 498.87 USD (US Dollars) per capita, Switzerland's GDP per capita- 84, 815.41 USD — World Bank Information (2013). Trillions of economy with an handful/little population means altogether different to trillions economy for 1.5 billion population (minimum projected by 2025 for India).

132. Religion is no more just a spiritual activity but has become an immense economic activity. When once anything becomes an economic activity a nexus of whole range of people is formed.

133. One way of stating our problems is, India has only 2.4% of worlds geographical land but 18% of worlds population. Per capita availability of arable land is declined to 0.13 ha and still decreasing. Heterogeneity of population is another serious problem. 134 crores plus divided into 7 major religions and numerous faiths and cults, 3000 castes and 25000 subcastes, 22 languages (on currency one finds only 15) , nearly 2000 dialects, 29 states and 7 union territories. With everybody asserting and trying not to just survive but climb up the ladder as much as possible, corruption, conflicts and pollution are inevitable consequences. Added to this are disputes with neighbouring countries.

134. Smart cities should not mean only constructing beautiful buildings, flyovers etc, They should provide good drainage facilities and water harvesting facilities, rehabilitate slum people and pavement dwellers in some better places, remove vendors and hawkers encroaching the footpaths and the roads and place them in a separate shopping complex constructed for them, avoid constructions in lands which were once water bodies, lay some gardens, widen the roads where required, redesign the old parts of the cities/towns which are crowded and has many extremely narrow lanes and by lanes, remove open drainage systems, create adequate and proper waste disposal facilities, construction of more public toilets, construction of spacious bus stands both for local transport and intercity transport, redesigning the lodges which are in a bad shape, decongestion of

cities etc. Governments and general public should think on these lines.

135. In 2011—when he was 89 yrs old—V.S. Achyuthanandan of Kerala has almost won the election. Narrowly defeated. Otherwise he would have been a Chief minister from 89 yrs to 94 yrs! Subsequently he has won the election but did not become CM but only a minister with an important portfolio. Jyothi Basu would have continued at least up to 91 but he stepped down at 86. Politicians as per our constitution have no age limit. It is up to the public to fix either an age limit or a fixed number of tenures for politicians. They can always contribute to the state/nation remaining outside the chair as well. Let the chance be given to some others to be groomed in the chair. The society will be having more number of people with first hand experience and this is an asset to the society.

136. To what extent India has become capable of defending itself? History says we were ruled cumulatively for nearly thousand years by Muslims, British, French, Portuguese, Dutch, Danish apart from short term conquests by many more. Post Independence, we know what has happened in Indo-china war. Till today we had been importing arms at a huge cost to defend ourselves.

137. There is no defence available against nuclear weapons. In retaliation even if we use them both sides would be irreversibly destroyed. The price paid for such an act can be known only then. Having discovered the weapons and stock piled, one day or other; one person or other is very likely to use them. It is premature to presume that nuclear weapons will not be used. India is not yet a strong country to reckon with. One Prime Minister paid a price for sending

military to Sri Lanka. One Prime Minister paid a price for sending military into the golden temple in Amritsar. One Prime Minister paid price—probably-for Tashkent agreement (Lal Bahdur Shastri's death had been controversial). Probably Nehru also died because of an aftershock effect of Indo China war. Which PM will pay a price for Kashmir problem, time has to tell. India should strengthen its Defece research & Development not only to defend but also to predict/preempty foreign attacks.

138. The problem of migration to state capitals from the rest of the state is assuming serious proportions. Chennai (capital of Tamil Nadu) has 16% of the total Tamil Nadu population. Further there is also a serious problem of inter-state migration. Opportunities must be created in different states and also in rural areas as there is lot of rural migration too not only for education but also for employment.

139. Slum dwellers rehabilitation should be done in small phases as was done in China some time back. At different times, small segments of slum population may be temporarily shifted to another place and permanent houses constructed in the original place. Rehabilitation has to be done in phases.

140. If a man or a woman is not satisfied with each other they should fall apart but have no right to kill each other.

141. Great men does not mean that they do not have flaws. They may have more number of flaws and even greater flaws. Only difference is that, they have been found to be remarkable/exceptional/commendable in something for which they are acknowledged and rewarded.

## B. Education and Science & Technology

**(Note**— All relevant parameters with respect to educational institutes need to be rationalised. Academic sector also is affected by several problems. Many aspects of Education and Science & Technology have been appraised in the book "Thoughts on Higher Education", Klapaz Publications, New Delhi, 2015. Readers particularly the well educated and policy planners are recommended to read this book.)

142. In developed west science has many important goals. Two among them are generation of wealth and defence of the country. In India science has to go a long way before we catch up with the developed west.

143. Einstein said – "Human welfare alone must be the sole aim of all scientific endeavour and this one should not forget in the midst of one's equations ".. So our policy planners should accordingly decide the projects and fund.

144. All existing and aspiring policy planners, academicians of all backgrounds, Bureaucrats, Politicians, Entrepreneurs, NGO's (Non-governmental Organisations), various awards and honours and all apex bodies pertaining to Education and Science & Technology and Social welfare should seriously think on the key issues listed by UN (United Nations) Viz; Economic Growth and Sustainable Development; International Peace and Security; Development of Africa; Human Rights; Humanitarian Assistance; Environment; Health; Refugees; Gender Equality; Justice; International Relations; Nuclear, Chemical and Conventional Weapons Disarmament; Drug control, Crime Prevention and Counter-terrorism.

145. The way UGC (University Grants Commission, New Delhi) has made Environment as a compulsory

subject for all at UG (Under Graduate level), it is vital that students at all levels study to different depths the social problems of India and accordingly curriculum be designed.

146. Life consists of lifeless molecules. Ultimate ambition of scientists from various backgrounds is to create life in the laboratory by synthesising and putting all the required molecules together. CraigVenter, a highly reputed academician and entrepreneur and his team from USA has made and making immense contributions towards this grand endeavour.

147. Sometimes serious conflicts accelerate the developments in science & technology. Second world war is a good example. India with its numerous problems, inadequacy in self sufficiency and the need to become a power to reckon with should also be expected to make strides in the developments of science & technology.

148. A task for both students and parents is of planning after plus two (that is after 12 years of schooling). This is the turning point and most of the students are not able to get proper guidance at this stage, which is the most crucial time.

149. An international survey has revealed that in certain places, the prevalence of mental health problems is much higher in PhD students than in the rest of the population. Indian academicians have a social and moral responsibility to avoid such a situation. They contribute and are expected to contribute a lot. Hence the well being of PhD students is of paramount importance apart from moral considerations.

150. We require great creative scientists who can come out with a successful technology for converting seawater into fresh water using solar energy apart

from using solar energy for other purposes. Government should seriously think about this.

151. Left side of the brain (Left Hemisphere) coordinated the right side of the body and is concerned with logic such as in science and mathematics. Right side of the brain (Right Hemisphere) coordinates the left side of the body and is concerned with tasks involving creativity and arts. Neuroscience is a challenging field for scientists for so many reasons.

152. It appears professional education is the third largest black money generator in the country—40 thousand crores. Medical education alone 12 thousand crores. (a news paper article). To this you add a huge number of private arts and science colleges and schools. Don't the children/students know how they got admission into the above colleges? Don't they reflect how their parents got so much money to pay for them? Don't they know how much money they have paid and for how much money they got the receipt from the colleges?

153. One of the main reason for question paper leakages of common entrance exams is the cut throat competition for entering into various professional courses after Pre-University Course/Plus two.

154. Intentionally or unintentionally — but definitely unfortunately— UGC was extremely varied in its area requirement to start new universities from time to time. Keeping its present requirement, the remaining surplus land in the universities must be suitably diverted for other causes.

155. Higher education being a concurrent subject and UGC 's autonomy to universities, there is enormous scope for every state and every university in a state to function in its own way.

156. Human Genome sequencing is welcome. But they should create some interest in the sequencing projects by selectively choosing different categories of people for sequencing, namely, whiz kids, people with high longevities, transgenders, different ethnic groups etc.

157. GM (genetically modified) crops allowed by US but some European countries are not allowing them. And both are developed countries. So one of the important factors hindering the acceptance of GM crops in India is the non-acceptance of GM crops by some European countries. What the farmers want is crop insurance and assured supply of seeds at affordable price or free of cost as a subsidy or welfare measure.

158. When you want to pursue higher education don't be hasty. Know (a) how long you want to continue in higher education? (b) your total financial commitments including the hidden costs for the entire program. (c) When you want to take up a job? (d) When you want to settle in your personal life? (e) Whether you want to remain in India or want to go abroad either because of personal settlement or professional pursuit? (f) that different institutes start their admission process at different times and the quality of the training imparted in them is different (g) rules and regulations of the educational institute.

159. Even before humans evolved to chose between vegetarian and non-vegetarian food, nature has created animals who are exclusively plant eaters—called herbivorus.

160. A widely accepted fact is—High fibre diet reduces the risk of colon cancer, irritable bowel syndrome and cardiovascular diseases. Particularly the correlation between lack of fibre and colon cancer is seriously felt.

161. Internet access doesn't make us instant experts. When one retrieves something one may get a huge number of hits. To go through all of them, collate and analyze requires lot of time, effort, expertise, analytical skills etc. Further it is possible entire information is not available on the net.

162. Rate of plant photosynthesis increases with increase in carbon dioxide not only up to 400 ppm (approximate present atmospheric carbon dioxide concentration) but even beyond. So plant more trees.

163. How long bore well water can last? Water level will go further down and down, making it unsuitable. Currently some parts of India is facing this problem. It is also leading to fluorosis.

164. Comparing and contrasting with the other parts of the world and with others in the same country/society is a good starting point for further planning, progress and development.

165. Many negative impacts of green revolution are known no. So we should work on them and evolve strategies to overcome the negative impacts. Better late than never.

166. Hope ministry of AYUSH (Ayurveda, Yoga and Naturopathy, Unani, Siddha and Homoeopathy) will become serious to take advantage of our country's ancient wisdom in herbal medicine. In fact in ancient days Hindu kings had personal physicians and they were administering herbal medicine only. Long time back in foreign west an intelligent move has started, i.e to start a scientific journal called 'journal of ethnobotany' to know the medicinal flora in different countries. Recently knowledge of Chinese traditional herbal medicine has won a Nobel prize. Of course Chinese have validated their ancient wisdom on

modern scientific lines. So many allopathic drugs are plant derived. As development of a drug is a team work. Government should see that credit is duly apportioned among the team members. Green revolution, white revolution, missile technology, all are a product of team effort. But the general public do not know who all are involved. Only people at the helm of affairs are known as Government gives credit only to them. So naturally, things fall into the hands profit oriented private companies who can make a team work for the owner.

167. Drug controller of India is unable to control the parallel duplicate drug market operating.

168. There are limitations for students to come from all over India –29 states and 7 Union territories –to come to some states and pursue engineering & technology courses and other courses. Various State Governments and AICTE (All India Council for Technical Education) and other apex bodies of education should survey all states and union territories and decide where to approve further and how much to approve?

169. Negative results are as good to publish. Others will not take the same course and waste time and resources. So they should be eligible for publication. If a candidate gets negative results after spending 5 yrs in PhD, he should be allowed to publish the negative results, submit the thesis and get his degree. One should not pressurize the candidate to show positive results.

170. Gradually more and more components of academic activity are getting commercialized.

171. Rodents are a big problem. Different funding agencies are giving grants for projects concerned with rodent

control, but no practical outcome has come so far. Best way is to give considerable money incentive to all those who bring dead rats and hand over to municipality. They will develop their own methods and bring dead rats. This is a better approach for rodent control.

172. Long back Lester Brown of World Watch Institute, Washington gave lot of recommendations developing and less developed countries but they could not or did not follow them.

173. It appears only about 40% of people have access/or go to allopathy. The rest 60% go for alternative systems of medicine. All these 60% are not poor people. Among them are many who can afford allopathy and yet preferred to go for alternative systems of medicine. Ministry of AYUSH is to validate these systems on modern lines.

174. Can we draw Vice chancellors and Registrars and other officials of universities from wide variety of backgrounds? As there is so much of competition from whatever background they come, very likely theirs will be a political appointment based on social, economical and regional considerations.

175. Humans are concerned about their species extinction, not other species extinction. Whatever humans feel is conducive for their perpetuation they will continue to do it. We have to decide how to feed our huge population. India has 2.4% of worlds land but 18% of worlds population. May be we have to clear forests for growing either crops for human consumption or animal consumption. Besides, the forest land has other uses like constructing buildings, need for fire wood and wood for other purposes, laying connecting roads, building new townships etc. It is really a complex problem.

176. In many countries particularly in the developed west, private companies have their own in-house R & D's (Research and Development divisions). So they are very rigorous in their planning of research projects. They need an outcome sooner or later which can be commercialised. Unfortunately such goal oriented projects are not there / not made mandatory in public institutions barring exceptions.

177. Why do you consider humans as separate from nature. He is as much a part of the nature. Nature has created so many species in the past and subsequently humans. For nature man is just another species evolved over time. Why blame man for changing the nature?

     Scientifically speaking, even before humans came into this world, the world was changing for a very, very long time. Who is responsible for those changes in the world?

178. Those who market scientists inventions earn money than who made the inventions.

179. Medical tourism that is patients from other countries coming to India has increased. Secondly unlike in olden days VIPs and other influential and popular personalities are not going abroad for treatment but getting treated in our country.

180. In spite of all odds, one major driving force for people to do Ph.D. is; they hope to go abroad for a Post – Doctoral Fellowship and earn in dollars or Euros etc. But the question is, how many and for how long one can go abroad? And how ultimately they want to end up? Settle abroad permanently? Purchase a job in India by the money earned abroad? Be abroad till you get a job in India without any problem? etc.

181. India should generate as much statistics as possible and generate as much classified information as

possible pertaining to all sectors and on all aspects to create awareness among the public and to facilitate planning.

182. Teacher absenteeism in schools is supposed to be highest in India as per an international survey. However it has not been assessed in colleges and universities which is also very much required.

183. Adulteration of so many items is common in our country. It is said that adulteration has become so rampant that it has led to a shortage of adulterants and it has become inevitable to adulterate the adulterants!

184. Beware universities! Your land may be taken away! Once upon a time UGC and other apex bodies insisted on possessing certain area of land to set up universities. Accordingly they were set up. Subsequently the apex bodies reduced this area limit. Now a days far less amount of land is required to set up an university as compared to olden days. The present view point of the politicians is universities don't require so much of land as they are currently possessing.

185. China has ear marked a certain amount of land for agriculture to feed its population. India also should calculate such a figure and the cropping pattern.

186. It's very common to see mothers carrying babies with them on two wheelers and in buses riding speedily on bumpy roads. Pediatricians (Doctors specialised in child care) should duly advise the mothers.

187. Teaching outside the class room is a big business in India at school level, particularly at plus two level. Tuition centers, coaching centers are in plenty. Even university and college teachers are increasingly

getting involved with plus two, private colleges, distance education centers, different coaching centers etc. Hence there is a neglect of teaching in the respective institutes in which they are actually employed.

188. Every character has a genetic component. No gene or genes can express unless a favourable environment is there, and no environment can bring the desired effect unless the relevant combination of genes are present.

189. The three southern states of Andhra Pradesh, Tamil Nadu and Karnataka have a third of all Ph.D. enrolments in the country while Delhi, home to 26 universities, comes fourth. With its largest student population, Uttar Pradesh stands fifth, followed by Maharashtra in the sixth spot. Andhra Pradesh with 46 universities has enrolled the largest pool of 8, 212 doctoral candidates. Tamil Nadu with the largest number of 59 universities has 7, 995 candidates pursuing Ph.D. program. Karnataka is a close third with 7, 938 Ph.D. candidates. In all, 77, 798 candidates are currently pursuing research in subjects ranging from humanities to natural sciences and from medicine to agriculture. Is it possible to produce as many worthwhile Ph.D's as mentioned above? And to employ them suitably?

190. Research funding should be stopped to private institutes. Let them be concerned with with rolling out students and if they are interested in doing research let them get grants from private industries or international grants. Such attitude of getting grants should also be inculcated among the faculty from all elite institutions.

191. There is a cat in U.S. which is 27 years old equivalent to 125 years of human life!. Researching on the

biology of aging and longevity of such animals will throw light on human aging and longevity.

192. It's true that some/ few Indian universities send theses to faculty in foreign universities. Questions that arise are: (a) How many faculty from foreign universities send their theses to us!? (b) In what way the quality of the theses of an Indian university which sends theses to foreign universities are different from the theses which are not sent to foreign universities but only to native universities? Absolutely no difference to the knowledge and experience of many. (c) How many theses— out of the total — sent to foreign university received bad comments and graded as "not recommended"? Never or negligible. If at all so happens it can be safely ignored by the university and duly takes care of the theses evaluation otherwise. (d) The time taken to complete the evaluation process of a thesis in the universities varies incredibly a lot.

193. How can education can impart values, ethics and morals when education system itself is highly commercialised and corrupted!?

194. Many are totally against the employers insisting on recommendation letters/ testimonials. Let them screen the candidates in their own way and select.

195. Some of the Government fellowships of PhD students are 2.5 times to 3 times more as to what a newly joined faculty—even after a Ph.D.— gets in some Private/self financing colleges/ institutes! Of course the students can enjoy this only if their guides/ supervisors don't demand a cut from the fellowship of the research scholars for some reason or other.

196. Ethics and standards in research can't be maintained because of poverty (extreme shortage of funds), unrealistic demands on the faculty for appointments

and promotions, multiple responsibilities in the job and wrong appointments.

197. When human cloning was being discussed, churches started saying "man playing against God"! A scientist replied. We are not playing against God. Who is giving us this knowledge? It's God! So with the knowledge and understanding God is giving we are functioning accordingly and going ahead!

198. Everyone blames. VC (Vice Chancellor) but no one blames the candidates! Everyone blames a politician but no one blames the voters! Why?

199. During promotions a candidate is asked about so many credentials/contributions. But never the candidate is asked how many classes you have taken till date!?

200. The difference between the fairest European and a negro is just few micrograms of melanin pigment per cell.

201. In India parents are primarily responsible. For them tuitions and studying otherwise at home for chosen careers are more important neglecting their all round development. Of course teachers and educational system also are contributory factors as they leave a lot of burden on children and youngsters.

202. Recently there was an uproar about fraud scientific journals in the world where scientists publish their work by paying money. Indian scientists funded by Indian Government funding agencies also figure in that. Many Indian journals do not take money for publishing. Does this mean that research published in these journals is all genuine? Secondly many scientists do not prefer to publish in Indian journals as their rating is low at the global level and often they take unduly long time to take a decision to

publish. Above all in the interviews employers do not give importance to publications in Indian journals. Candidates are usually asked as to how many publications they have in International journals? If that is the attitude then why run journals by Indians? It is important to remember that though fraud journals take money and publish there are many reputed/genuine International journals who also take money for publishing papers.

203. Older generation- good, bad and worse have retired. Recruits in the new generation: (a) some are chips of the old blocks (b) others have been recruited because of socio, political and economic considerations. (c) very few by merit and they can't be close to the lobbies/ coteries. So the possibility of any good future for science in all categories of institutes is remote or at the most an insignificant amount of contribution may come.

204. Goals in terms of time dimensions maybe broadly divided into, short term, medium term, long term. Maybe someone may add very long term also. So what the first PhD does at the most falls under short term category. And if the first PhD is authentic and is continued further along the same goal, it may become a medium term goal and if continued further at the end of the 3rd or 4th Ph.D., the desired goal may be achieved. Unfortunately our guides/research supervisors do not (or can't?) stick to a goal for any appreciable length of time, leave aside till the end of the goal. They don't or can't work on a single aspect for a long time. Arthur kornberg apparently worked almost throughout his life only on DNA polymerase! Frederick Sanger, worked for a long time on protein sequencing and got a Nobel prize and then switched over to nucleic acid sequencing, worked for a long time and got a second Nobel prize! For both we may

just use the term, Macromolecular sequencing. There should be a continuity of work to accomplish a goal. For e.g. every plant breeder knows the time dimensions to develop a variety. So how can there be a new crop variety released for farmers without continuity of work for a long time? Can agricultural scientists accomplish this goal with the help of just one Ph.D. candidate? Bill gates- Melinda foundation has promised to fund for 12 to 15 years at IRRI (International Rice Research Institute), Philippines, for accomplishing the goal of conversion of C3 crops to C4 crops- rice to be specific. In India where most of it is public funding we have a moral binding on goal oriented mandates. Unfortunately it's not there. Government should ponder over this.

205. It is common that after western scientists report something, within no time our scientists also report and claim a similar finding. A few times unfortunately it so happens that after sometime the westerners claim is found to be a hoax and even their published research papers are retracted. That is where our Indian scientists are caught! Our scientists keep mum and the institutes in which the scientists are working also do not take any action on our scientists.

206. In this context another anecdote may be said. Malthus –famous British scholar—said in the past that population increases in geometric progression while food production increases in arithmetic production. Simply stated food production cannot keep pace with the population increase. So our scientists also use to say the above. Subsequently Green revolution took place with an immense surge in food production. Westerners started saying that science & technology has defeated Malthusian theory. Soon our scientist also started saying so! With

passing time population was growing a lot and westerners have started saying "the ghost of Malthus is till haunting us". So our scientists also started saying so and so on....!

207. In the present system neither one can be an honest and competent teacher nor an honest and competent researcher. Forget about remaining as both.

208. (a) If according to some, teaching is carried out by incompetent teachers, some say it's a better situation that is prevailing! At least teacher is coming to the class to cover the syllabus to the extent of his ability. He is an honest teacher though may be incompetent, because he is at least coming to handle the classes. Many are not unaware or do not point out intentionally that there is considerable teacher absenteeism in educational institutions. Whether competent or incompetent the teacher doesn't come to the class or comes occasionally or comes not to deliver the lecture but to listen to the students lecture on the syllabus topic which has been given as a seminar assignment.

(b) Whose duty it is to see that the teachers are going to the classes? Dean? Registrar? Or VC (Vice Chancellor)? None does this monitoring. And the above, when they were teachers they never probably handled classes or only occasionally. So they prefer their breeds. How about parents? They are scared of any consequence to their wards. Hence do not complain.

209. Once some gave an idea; let us pool all the big shots in the country and place all of them in a single institute so that we can make at least one world class institute. That did not materialize because -it was simply not possible--they cannot coexist. They cannot see eye to eye each other. Each big shot wants to build/wants to have his/her own empire.

210. Once a question was asked by an eminent director of a very reputed institute in India. The question is, are we Tall among Talls or are we Tall among Dwarfs? He concluded that we are Tall among Dwarfs. So all our scientists in reputed institutes also come under the above category. Let us hope one day we will really be classified as Tall.

211. Our problem is to provide food for 134 crore plus people and still increasing. So we have to grow staple crops. Again there is a preference here of different people. Many want to eat only rice and wheat. Very few want to teat coarse grains—Raagi, Baajra, Sorghum etc. The need for water and other inputs accordingly vary. When you want to grow only rice, wheat and sugar cane in a huge way, water requirements are very high. Cropping pattern should be decided according to the needs of the society and according to the affordability of the required inputs. That does not happen.

212. Problems of agriculture in India are more complicated. (a) need to feed a huge population, that too according to their preferences (b) diversion of land from staple crops to commercial crops (c) decreasing availability of land and water and water is required not only for agriculture but also for drinking etc. (d) encroachment of lakes and other water bodies. (e) Poor drainage and water conservation. (f) decrease in the number of people who want to remain in farming. (g) Increase in the prices of real estate/farm land. Farmers are happy to sell away their land and are able to afford their children to get into education and job. Giving kick back is not a problem for them anymore as the land prices are high. Who once upon a time were called poor/marginal farmers have suddenly became rich because of increase in prices of real estate/farm land. Father can sell away 1-3

acres of land and settle his son and /or his daughter. Subsequently they will take care of the parents. Price of the farm land varies from 20 lakhs to 2 crores per acre—and even 5 crores— depending on the place. (h) Shortage of farm labour because of industrialisation and migration. (i) automation not always suitable to small holdings. (j) reluctance of farmers to do collective farming.

213. One cell is approximately one nanogram. Therefore 70kg person has 70 trillion cells. However there are other ways of calculating the number of cells. Secondly we do not take into account the number of microbial cells in and on our body which are a huge number.

214. Indians have been using neem for a long time. But the credit for azadirachtin (active chemical isolated from neem) goes to somebody else. It's true with so many other plants. We always remained empirical and still we are. So others are bound to take credit for everything.

215. One of the important original objectives of establishing agricultural universities was; a good number of students would come from farming families get formally educated in agriculture and would return back to their farming. But the truth is rarely it happened. All have opted for different jobs. So agriculture universities require a tailor made manpower planning in every state. And since a large number of agricultural institutes come under central government they too require a similar planning.

216. Once there was an uproar about government doctors being busy in their private practice neglecting the duties in the government hospitals. In support of them they said. When teachers neglect their duties in their respective government schools and colleges

and become busy giving tuitions at different places and in coaching centres, why not we do private practice?

217. A loan is taken by a country or given to a country by someone with the expectation that the loan would be wisely utilized to come up and make enough money for themselves and also be in a position to pay back the loan. Loan has to be treated as an investment given to the country (or as a temporary relief for some crisis, which the country may hope to tide over soon). Unfortunately it may not happen. Many of the science grants/ loans from abroad seem to have gone waste. From these grants we could not develop products, goods and services and commercialize.

218. Our incapability to be self sufficient and dependence on foreign countries has made them remain in a win situation. One defence deal can drain out so much of our money (foreign reserves). Apart from defence we are also dependent on import of several other items. The country should be clear about why it's taking a loan and aftermath. So blaming the foreign countries in a blanket manner always does not serve the purpose. We cannot right now predict to what extent we can become self sufficient because of the slogan "Make in India" by Honorable PM.

219. Japan and Germany, were well advanced even before they were devastated by world war. It's a different story, they lost the war. (As philosophy says, defeat and victory are in the hands of Almighty.) So it was not difficult for them to bounce back. India was not scientifically (modern science) as advanced as Japan and Germany, even if we compare ourselves to their advancement before their devastation. Before world war Japan and Germany were not conquered and ruled like us by many invaders for nearly 950 years.

Further they are a highly homogeneous lot. We are a tremendous and an incredible mixture of people and overpopulated.

220. It's simply not possible to have quality teachers. Even those who have the potential to become a quality teacher does not care for teaching. The reason is everything is decided on the basis of research credentials — appointments at all levels, promotions till professor from the entry level, securing grants from funding agencies, securing higher posts at different levels in different organisations, securing awards and honors etc — all take into account primarily research credentials of a person. So a person concentrates on how to build up research credentials—by all means— and this hardly leaves any time or even no time for teaching. Even the best teacher award is decided on the basis of research credentials!! Teaching is a thankless job. No one wants to do it.

221. Highly skewed funding is a characteristic feature in the education and science & technology sector.

227. When you spray air freshener/perfume in your room or any other enclosed space, the unpleasant odour is only masked. Otherwise the substances which were earlier giving unpleasant odour are very much still there in the ambience. And we continue to breathe them. In case they are toxic we face the consequences. The freshener/perfume just masks the odour. It no way detoxifies the unwanted substances in the air.

228. In India it's all the more common. It's the science administrators and science managers who take the credit rather than the workers. Those who confer the credit dishonestly on a single or a very few persons should also be considered guilty.

229. We have a huge student population. Diversification of careers is one solution to make them employable. The government definitely can't give jobs to everyone in the same field.

230. There are 6728 enzymes— as on May 23, 2016—!

231. Babies in olden times were fed by mothers for a much longer time. Were they unscientific and the babies in any way undernourished and lagged in development then?

232. Since ages it is known. When any country invades another country soldiers rape women of the invaded country. And we have a huge number of War Babies. In the present day we can identify the parent by DNA finger Printing. Hence the genome Data bank of all soldiers be made mandatory and maintained. And when the necessity arises war babies genome can be matched with the stored data bank and the father identified and accordingly take suitable measures thereafter. All this requires lot of money and insistence from UNO (United Nations Organisation) to follow the procedure.

### C. Philosophy and Religion (PR)

233. Different denominations (divisions/affiliations) in the same religion exist in all major religions.

234. Both scientists and philosophers believe that there was a time when human being was not there and there will be again a time when human being will not be there on earth.

235. Even In modern drug trials placebo (benefit due to psychological effect rather than physiological effect of the drug) works up to 20%. So religious prescriptions also may work to a certain extent in the same manner. One cannot know whether one falls

under that lucky percentage when following religious prescriptions! No harm in following if one can.

236. In Hindu temples people are not allowed to enter with footwear. But in west people enter church with shoes and in houses also. In India because of their ancient Hindu tradition even Christians in many places do not enter church with footwear. So one cannot say that those who are entering churches with foot wear are blasphemous or God will punish them.

237. In no religion reward for good things or punishment for bad things is said/guaranteed to be received in this very life. You may get it in next or next to next birth etc according to Hinduism and Buddhism etc which believes in multiple births and after the end of the world —Last day of Judgement according to the three Abrahamic religions.

238. Kazuo Ishiguro from Japan has won the Nobel prize for literature in 2017. The citation of the Nobel Academy "He has uncovered the abyss beneath our illusory sense of connection with the world" brought happiness to many philosophers.

239. Did God has given man immense free will to make faults or not to make faults!? How much amount of freewill God has given to man? Has he given equal amount of freewill to every man?

240. Doesn't God have any obligation towards his creatures? If so what is wrong in expecting from him? Since we believe he has the power to grant anything, what is wrong in praying him and expecting something?

241. Kaliyuga supposed to have started 3102 years BC. Before that is dwaapar yug supposed to have lasted for 8, 64, 000 yrs and before that is Thretha Yug when Ram was there. So time records are different according to Hindu calendar.

242. Religious and cultural custodians should maintain adequate and authentic records/archives. Tampering of religious literature in many ways can occur and if so one should be able to detect them and separate from the original. Eternal vigilance on the part of every one is very much essential to prevent religion from unscrupulous distorters.

243. When we become helpless and cannot come out on our own, when no rescue comes from any side and when human help is missing, when there is no hope from any side, there is no other go, than to look towards God. It is natural.

244. Someone said..Oh! God. You need not have to give me anything. Just appear before me once. (the man's belief is if he can have a look at him, that's sufficient to get whatever he wants). Adi Shankaracharya prayed to God once. I don't mind what you throw at me. If your intention is only to trouble me, no problem. But kindly appear before me and say so. I'll be happy!

245. Even psychiatrists recommends God, Prayer etc. They acknowledge the positive effect of them. It is said but for God we may require one psychiatrist in every colony.

256. Religion is not something left over from the infancy of our intelligence. It's something emanated from highly matured minds. Those who have preached religion earlier are not men of any inferior intelligence. It may fade away as reflected in the increased number of atheists population in the world. But it will never die and it will get re-established with principles of greater universal applicability. The course of human life is such that religion can never die. It will remain alive.

257. Philosopher Aurobindo said "Great saints have performed miracles. Greater saints have railed at them. Greatest saints have both performed and railed at them".

258. Dr. S. Radhakrishnan, former president of India and renowned comparative philosopher said-religions must be cured of their provinciality and must be made to reveal their universality.

259. End of the world or God returning in future is there in Hinduism, Islam and Christianity.

260. Even by theistic definition God is beyond human comprehension. We can know infinitesimally little about him. That is why we repose faith in those whom we believe as highly elevated souls—who have relatively a greater knowledge of God — and follow what they say irrespective of our spiritual status.

261. Many religions give a masculine attribute to the Almighty/God. In Hinduism GOD can be masculine, feminine or even neutral i.e, He, She or It. All are right. We have deified everything and represented God in many forms.

262. Ekam sat vipra bahudha vadhanthi (एकं सतविप्र बहुधा वदन्ति)— Truth is one but sages tell it in different ways-—problem is with the second part—bahudha vadhanthi. —different ways--it became so much varied that people started fighting saying that "our basic tenets/principles are different from yours". And subsequently serious divisive tendencies arose.

263. Man suffers because of 3 reasons. (i) because of his own code of conduct termed as Aadhyatmika (आध्यात्मिक) (ii) because of others—both fellow human beings and other animals. In olden days people used to travel through jungles and get killed by wild animals. Getting killed by snake bites was also

common, happening till recently and even today we hear such cases. Similarly getting killed by dog bites. Though they were aware of deaths because of pox and microorganisms, they never made a separate mention. This suffering is called... Aadhibhouthika (आदि भौतिक) — that's because of all other organisms from fellow human beings to microbes. iii) because of God himself..termed as –Aadhidhaivika (आदि देविका). e.g. natural disasters like earthquakes etc. To what extent the above three causes can be avoided? Answer varies from 0 to 100 percent. It's a perennial debate.

264. Chinese celebrate —the year of Monkey. In India we worship Hanuman in the form of monkey routinely.Many feel that it is absolutely wrong to depict Hanuman with a monkey morphology/figure. Hanumaan, Vaali, Sugreeva, Angadha—all have communicated/conversed with Rama (राम), Raavana (रावण), Seetha (सीता) and others. Had they been monkeys, it was impossible to communicate/converse so. It is widely believed that Hanuman also has written a Ramayana (there are many who have written Ramayana). A monkey cannot write Ramayana.

So it is absolutely wrong to refer to the above as vaanaras (वानर) or vaanara sena (वानर सेना) as monkeys in the ordinary sense. They are very likely just another social group. Social groups may their emblems/totems. So very likely the truth is, a particular social group had a monkey as their emblem/totem. Hence they are addressed as vaanaras (वानर) or vaanara sena (वानर सेना) and depicted also in a monkey form. Now can we change the idol of Hanuman into a human form? Impossible to imagine.

Our brains are so much conditioned to worship hanuman in a monkey form.

265. OM is a sound and not a letter to be reflected upon.

266. Gregor John Mendel-father of Genetics— was a monk. So one can be religious and still do great science. But what motivated him to do study genetics? How he planned and carried out so many experiments for such a long time? All the characters he has chosen were located on different chromosomes of the pea plant he has chosen to work! A miracle. Nothing to be criticised if one says that God has given him the knowledge.

277. Often people quote supreme court which has declared that "Hinduism is a way of life". Not so. It has simply stated what Dr. S. Radhakrishnan, philosopher and president of India stated. Dr Radhakrishnan used this expression—not because he does not give credence to the basic tenets/ principles of Hinduism—but keeping in view the wide variety of practices prevailing under the umbrella of Hinduism in this vast country of high social heterogeneity. The above expression—a way of life— was very much liked by other religions too and they started using for them.

278. Theists will be defeated if they start saying "Our God" "Your God" and "Their God". Hope one day they realise that there is only one God and act accordingly. That will benefit the entire humanity.

279. Science says neither matter nor energy can be created or destroyed. But they can be transformed into each other. From where/how they have emanated? Initially what was there? Matter or Energy or both? If so in what proportions? Rationalists don't agree that something has come from nothing. Now if you say that this something has come from that. then the person would ask form where that has come?

Say, you point out to something else. The questioning continues. Is there any end to such questioning? So the inevitable conclusion is, in the beginning there was something all by itself from which everything else has emanated. You may call that something anything you like. But this is the only conclusion one can arrive at after exhausting all the questions and answers.

280. We cannot explain the universe without bringing God into picture. Stephen hawking surrendered saying, don't ask me beyond bang. But how can one stop questioning further? And there is no end to that. So it is inevitable to bring God into picture. Einstein said - everything in this universe is going on in such a perfect manner, there must be a super mathematician behind the universe. An obvious reference to the existence of God.

281. Some of our custodians of religion have the habit of converting/ projecting every powerful personality, sooner or later as.some avathara (an incarnation of some God or other or born because of a specific blessing of God etc) . Of course there are always people to follow what has been said. But such fabrications have a negative effect on the credibility of the religion in the eyes of others including Hindu population.

282. There were/are many Ghost writers for many God men.

283. If desires merge in you there is no problem. But if you want to merge with the desires it is a catastrophe. —Bhagvatgita.

284. In panchathanthra stories written by Vishnu Sharma, so many animals are talking. One is not asked to believe that different animals are really communicating/ conversing with each other! One is

to concentrate on the take home message and the moral of the story. The same thing holds good for mythology too.

285. The harsh fact is, death is not just a painful truth but a highly uncertain truth. When and how a person dies is different from person to person. The diversity of human beings is matched only by the variety of deaths that await them. Starting from 'still births' (dying in the womb itself) to hundred plus we find people dying in variety of ways.

286. One extreme opinion is there is no soul, even for human beings. Another extreme is, every living being, plants, animals, humans, microorganisms- all have souls. A third group says only humans have souls but not all other living beings mentioned above.

287. Hindu philosophy says that one should live like the water/ drop of water on a lotus. You know the drop of water remains on the lotus leaf but doesn't get attached to it. So that is how one is recommended to live in the world.

288. Prey and predator relationships are created by nature / God. We cannot do anything. What is prey to one is a predator of something else. All these have to hunt for food and the preys have to defend from being hunted. That is how nature is.

289. There are numerous stories of —from rags to riches. But as a percentage of total they are negligible. That is why some people talk about the Grace of God in such cases.

Raja Bhirthruhari said. अगर माथे पे लिखा है वो चव्वनी हो या अरब हो अगर आप रेगिस्तान में भी रहोगे तो आपको मिल जायेगा (if you are destined to get –whether it is a pittance or immense wealth –you would get it even if you are living in a desert). A good example for Raja Bhirtruhari's quote is Guelph countries people in desert area living in modest conditions. On one fine day God made them to discover oil treasures. They never dreamt about it. Now they are unimaginably rich and a power to reckon with in the world.

290. Many believe that there had been a large amount of tampering of various sorts with our ancient literature. Hence what we have today needs to be critically viewed.

291. Knowledge and spirituality are two different things. A knowledgeable man need not be spiritual and vice versa.

292. How one is supposed to understand Bhagawath geetha? Who preached Bhagawath geetha? Krishna श्री क्रिशन). To whom Krishna preached? To Arjuna (अर्जुन). So how one is supposed to understand Bhagawath geetha? One is supposed to understand Bhagawath geetha the way Krishna expected Arjuna to understand. Isn't? How did Arjuna understood and acted? This is how one should analyze. Rest is superfluous.

**D. Quotes and Quips (QQ)**

293. An old joke— A staunch atheist came to India and travelled throughout and on way back he said he started believing in God! He remarked-Who else is running this country? It is only God!

294. An old anecdote— There is no retirement for lawyers—only death or facial paralysis! However politicians seems ot have a better advantage. For lawyers only in private practice age is not a bar. But politicians can form a part of the government. Age bar does not apply to them.

295. Satirical definitions (a) Repartee— A reply in retort. Practiced by all gentlemen who have a constitutional aversion for violence but a strong disposition to offend. (b) Selfish— One who is devoid of consideration for other's selfishness.

296. Very old joke reflecting the state of affairs in the country. Story of three class fellows Brightest one after finishing his engineering degree became an engineer in the PWD department. Lesser one appeared for IAS, got cleared and became Secretary in the same PWD dept. Least of all joined politics and became a PWD minister. (I have expanded the above as follows: the fourth class fellow –worst among all the four—pursued PhD in some subject and subsequently became a professor).

297. A large number of hitherto religious have become atheists and agnostics in different parts of the globe. And many more on the way. An interesting thing is, the functioning of the theists differs only slightly from the atheists and agnostics. Only difference is they devote some time to God.

298. Oscar Wilde —There are only two tragedies in life. One is not getting what you want and another is to get it!

299. A weak man has no other go than to forgive. A weak man forgiving has no relevance. And a strong man seldom forgives.

300. After Jesus Christ, Marx is the second Jew who has influenced many people in the world. The original Jews who are following their ancient religion Judaism are strangely very few in the world.

276. In some parts of the country boys are not getting married as their hoses do not have a toilet! A lady refuses to marry a person in whose house there is no

toilet. It's said India is a country which has more mobiles and less toilets. Not just that. If Government asks the members of a house hold whether they want a toilet or a mobile as a welfare measure, they prefer only mobiles! Such is the psyche.

277. Sleep is a God's gift. Sleep as much as you can and as long as you can. It bestows both physical and mental health.

278. USSR has broadly two groups of population. European and non- European. Many feel whatever may be the form of government, the European population are likely to be better off than the non European populated regions.

279. Francis Bacon — Where there is fear, there is hatred .

280. Entire India looks beautiful staying abroad!

281. Everyone wants to own a car — very long and very broad and which can travel at high speeds. But no one is bothered about the width of the roads and the condition of the roads!

282. Govt. wants to introduce a paper on anti-corruption in the students curriculum. Who is going to be the faculty in charge for teaching the course paper on anti-corruption? Most likely the one who got into the job otherwise!

283. It seems when Einstein breathed his last, he spoke in German and the nurse by the side of him doesn't know German. So last words of Einstein are not known! .

284. While there are many cases of serendipity (accidental discoveries) in science, never it happens with Indians nor we get anything in the dreams like the scientist Kekule who discovered the structure of aromtic ring..

Though Pasteur may be right in saying-- fortune favors a prepared mind- it appears serendipity favoured even those without a prepared mind.

285. Nostradamus prophecies since decades about many events happening in India were being published. It's all fake. You insist. Any person making prophecies on the basis of Nostradamus, ask him to simultaneously provide the original French verses of Nostradamus. All French knowing people both in India and abroad, both common men and academicians can make out what it's. Veracity (truth) or the sensibility of extrapolation from the original French verses can be established.

286. A stubborn man is more powerful than God.

287. The family that eats and prays together stays together.

288. Many Indians know very well that they cannot change the state of affairs in the country and there is no other go than to change themselves. It is really a lot of pain constantly changing with the changing scenario!.

289. It is the inherent nature of the mind to become many times restless, wayward, incoherent etc. It's normal with most. That's why one philosopher said—. Mind is a monkey. Let it run. But you don't run after the monkey.

290. Philosopher Khalil Gibran said — you can only give your love to your children but not your thoughts. For they have their own thoughts. Today it's more true. He further said. Children come through you but they do not belong to you. (This reflects a view point of Hindu philosophy)

291. Academicians rubbing the back of other academicians is a very old phenomenon. It was termed as--society

for mutual appreciation—Politicians entry to an undesirable extent is relatively a recent phenomenon. For this, again academicians only are to be blamed as it is they who rope in politicians into academic affairs. Once a highly qualified politician was asked. Sir you're a reputed academician why did you join politics ? He replied. "There are more politics in academics than in politics. So I preferred politics".

292. Viraat roop (विराट रूप) / vishwaroopam (विश्व रूप) / Cosmic form which Lord Krishna has shown to Arjuna during Mahabharat war. As we see in photos and calendars etc Lord Krishn's/ Vishnu's face in the center and faces of so many Gods/ deities on either side. But you don't find a single face of a goddess / female diety!?

293. Time can turn friends into foes and foes into friends.

294. True Vegans don't consume even milk!

295. It's difficult to understand Chinese because of their traditional wisdom of pretending foolish!

296. Once a person was lecturing about the glories of God for a long time and in great appreciation said to the audience. Is there anything which God can't do ? Someone from the audience stood up and said...God can't please everyone.

297. Deification is probably a mental weakness of many Hindus. They deify everything, animate and inanimate. Is there anything in Hindu religion which is not a God ?. Latest addition probably is milestones on the road sides ! Smear vermillion (सिंदूर/लाल रंग), turmeric (हल्दी), Vibhuti (विभूति) etc, put a small garland of flowers. People stop at the milestones and bow with folding hands.

298. Whiz kids.—India has a couple of them in music and mathematics. (a). Scientific explanation is inexplicable mutations. (b). Hindu philosophical explanation—-residual knowledge from the previous birth being manifested.

299. Owners of media seem to have strong affiliations to different ideologies. Hence they lack professionalism and integrity in conveying to the public real analysis and real reporting. This problem seems to be there even in olden days which made Mark twain to say..."if you don't read a news paper you are not informed and if you read you are misinformed". Same situation in India.

300. Gandhi ji told long back that the world doesn't know us the way we identify ourselves but only as Indians. But today the whole world has a detailed analysis of Indian census.

301. Lower court, high court, supreme court. We have in all 6 lawyers and 3 judges. Law is the same. Yet we may have three different judgements.

302. The factor of luck is evident in many cases.

303. There is a site on Facebook— Atheist Republic. It is worth reading for theists too. They can then sound more rationale. Rationale theists are more likely to be accepted by a larger section of the society and is probably more good to the society.

304. In psychiatry/ psychology terms, daughters attachment to fathers and sons attachment to mothers is termed as Oedipus complex.

305. (a). Be a thief but don't preach others to become so. (b). Do as I say, don't do as I do.

306. Criticism on Indian scientists. They work on topics like for e.g. effect of cosmic radiation on the sex life

of ants ! We have limitations to do crazy science in view of fulfilling the needs of a huge population and of defending the country. We want highly imaginative people to do science to fulfil the above objectives more effectively, economically and speedily. Not to take whimsical projects.

307. For our country we require a) an akshaya paathra (अक्षयपात्र)—a celestial vessel which can supply inexhaustible food. b) a kaamadhenu (कामधेनु)—a divine cow which provides whatever one desires—- and c) a kalpavriksham (कल्पवृक्ष)—wish fulfilling divine tree. All the three are mentioned in Hindu mythology. Even after possessing them, we keep fighting as to where they should be placed ? People will demand a rotational policy among the 29 states and 7 union territories. And for the sake of possessing them there will be a demand for the creation of more states. Even if God is merciful for e.g. to give an akshaya paathra, people continue to fight that the same akshaya paathra (अक्षयपात्र) should not be used to get vegetarian food, non-vegetarian, beef and pork. So we may demand God to give different akshaya paathras!!. It is an established historical fact that the term Hindu etc was coined by others and not by us. But all got stuck to it - even today we are accustomed to use the words, Hindu and Hinduism. Right reference is sanatani (सनातनी) and sanatan Dharm (सनातन धर्म).

308. Can you define. What is Morality? How to differentiate Moral and Immoral? Morality is a matter of time and convenience. What is Moral and what is Immoral varies with time, place, society, circumstance, country, religion —all these variables decide what is moral and not.

309. How long we can/want to bask in the past glory. We must be concerned with the present state of affairs of the country to come up.

310. A baby is in fact not interested in the mother. Baby wants to be fed. It's immaterial for the baby whether mother feeds or some other lady feeds. In fact baby cannot even differentiate which lady is capable of feeding and which lady is not. Baby's attention is only on the bosom of the lady..

311. The words of the poor are profitless, though they may be sound in thought and clear in expression. (Tiruvalluvar-Tamil saint Kural, 1046).

312. Butterfly struggles to come out of the cocoon. A kind person but who couldn't understand the nature's way of doing things, thought he has to reduce the struggle of the butterfly. So he made a hole in the cocoon for the butterfly to easily come out. It so happened but the butterfly has lost its ability to fly !.

313. I'm happy people have misunderstood me. I would have been in for a lot more trouble had they understood me."

314. India's air pollution in 2050. A person got fainted. His family took him to a doctor. Doctor examined and said everything is OK. He just happened to breath pure air somehow!

315. A large number of atheists and agnostics are prospering. (So belief in God is not necessary for prospering).

316. It's a Paradox. World is so heavily populated..7. 9 billion people and India 134 crores plus. Yet a large number suffer from loneliness! Something wrong with the society.

317. They alone live who live by agriculture, all others are a cringing dependent life. Agriculture, though

laborious is the most excellent. All others have to resort to the farmer. (Thiruvalluvar Tamil saint Kural, 1033 & 1031). Paradox is those who think on these lines and remain in agriculture are decreasing with time.

318. Fortunately, unlike in olden days, now we have mobiles, Facebook, email, Skype, which helps to reduce the sadness. Leave aside friends, children go abroad and don't meet even their parents, kith and kin from one to few years. And their visit to India will be only for a short time. They go back again not to meet them for some more years.

319. Unfortunately/ unwisely Japan attacked different countries in the past. Had they not done it and confined themselves to the development of their own country, they would have emerged as another super power in the world.

320. Don't be idealistic to the detriment of practicality and don't be practical to the detriment of idealism. Do not be practical to the detriment of being sentimental and do not be sentimental to the detriment of being practical.

321. Things can change in minutes. Think of earthquakes or dropping of an atomic bomb.

322. Nowadays a stupid is one who cannot/ does not want to amass wealth.

323. Whatever that is destined to you, it will be come back to you even if you throw away. (Whatever that is not destined cannot be retained whatever efforts you make to retain it.-Tamil Saint Tiruvalluvar, Kural 376 ).

324. Banning corruption should take priority over banning of tobacco and alcohol. UN analyzing evils of the developing countries said with respect to India—

corruption and population— are the twin evils. Of corruption UN said it is AIDS of democracy.

325. The concept of family and prohibited relations is of recent times in terms of human civilization.

326. No one could answer the question. Why an all merciful, omnipotent God should create so much misery, pain and struggle ?

327. In the present times in view of developments in medical science & technology it is quite valid to ask "Who is the mother"? 1. One who donates the egg? 2. One who gives the mitochondria? 3. One who gives the womb? 4. One who feeds the child? As per todays science & technology and exceptional situations arising one may require four different ladies to get a child born and fed.

328. Capitalists say—it still require guns to maintain peace. Communists say—Power flows through the barrel of the gun. Any big difference ? 315. Neither your bank account nor anybody's heart can come to one's rescue if nature is not generous. 316. Both Chanakya and Marcus Aurelius said...in politics ends are important, not the means.

329. God has no phone, but he can listen to everyone and in every language. He has no Facebook but he is a friend to all. He doesn't have Twitter but he follows every one. And he doesn't bother even if one is an atheist. He still remains the same.

330. If the king is unjust, there will be no rains. (Tiruvalluvar-Tamil saint, Kural, 559). But in democracy who is the king ? The voter ! So it is his injustice that is responsible for not getting rains!

331. Some time back. Industrialists both from India and foreign expressed that they don't mind paying money/ bribes. But pleaded to make the entire thing...

"a single window system'. That's, one pays just at one place and the work is done. But it didn't work. Because Indian system has so many windows that too of different sizes and at different places. Then industrialists came with the idea of establishing a liaison office with a liaison officer. So he/ they take care of every window and complete the job.

332. Natural or man made disaster ? In India. There is one death every four minutes due to a road accident in India. Over 1,37,000 people were killed in road accidents in 2013 alone, that is more than the number of people killed in all our wars put together.

333. Arise, awake and stop not, till the goal is reached.... Swami Vivekananda.

334. Sometimes one single mistake or one single unfortunate incident may change the whole course of life. We live enduring.

335. Those who predict election results are called psephologists. Often they go wrong. Because they do not fully understand about vote bank politics, electoral arithmetic, effect of poll promises etc.

336. Green revolution has severely depleted the organic matter of the soil. Sustainable development advocate organic farming. In U.S. organic farming products are one and half times to two times expensive. In India also there will be enough buyers for the entire produce paying such high prices. Netherlands was once ready to export tonnes of dung. But what one should realise is, organic farming cannot feed the huge population of India.

337. There is a saying...men and nations do behave wisely when once all other alternatives are exhausted. Even if that is so, no problem. We wait till then. But Indians and India seem to function in a different way.

After exhausting all the alternatives they restart with the first, going through the cycle once again. So we can never become wise.

338. Someone said that Saudi doesn't have a single river. How it's coping up with its water requirements?

339. Not only academicians and other intellectuals in the society but even Godmen are skeptical about the future of our country. And this is really demoralising. Once a Godman told that when some Indians went to Lord Brahma and asked, when our country would be better off, he took more time than what Indians expected and finally said—Not in my life time (approx. 10.5 billion years—remaining life time of Lord Brahma according to one estimate)! Hope good sense dawns on us and we prevent a painful future.

340. Nowadays a talent is considered as a talent or useful only if you can commercialize it.

341. Every idea has to come from west/UN organisations. We are incapable of generating ideas beneficial to our country.

342. Both Chanakya and Kautilya seems to have said that for a person who is handling honey, some amount of it sticks to his fingers! (said so, with respect to persons in charge of treasury. In other words the person will definitely swindle some money from the treasury). So we had a long tradition of corruption. Subsequently foreign invasions, increase in population, increase in the need for huge number of goods and services etc have made large number of people becoming corrupt.

343. Laughing even without reason also has a therapeutic value. Psychologists recommend so. .

344. Nobel prize (2015) in economics is given to Professor. Angus Deaton for his analysis of 'consumption,

poverty, welfare and progress in India and china". Strange that no Indian economists has worked on these lines in his own country to come up to the level of claiming a Nobel Prize. Our problems are studied and analysis is given by westerners. Naturally it follows that recommendations and solutions also will be given by them to us. This is probably true on other issues related to India.

345. The suffering that fools inflict on themselves is hardly possible even to foes. (Tiruvalluvar Tamil saint Kural, 843).

346. No farmer wants his son to be in farming but prefers him to be a computer scientist. So how can you have green India before digital India ?

347. When you lose everything what you gain is experience! And by then it is too late to aim for success.

348. A man with money is young, handsome and can sing well too and respected. Raja Bhartruhari said सर्वेगुणाः काञ्चनमाश्रयन्ति—i.e all good attributes are conferred upon a man when once he acquires wealth even if he actually does not possess them.

349. When expectations are not fulfilled, it leads to anger. Anger leads to confusion, confusion leads to loss of memory, loss of memory leads to loss of reason and because of loss of reason you perish. (Bhagawath Geetha).

350. Who knows? The worst is yet to come? Present is probably better. So don't take future for granted.

351. Pollution cannot be stopped. It's an inevitable consequence of population and progress.

352. What brain implants our ancients had to store in memory the entire religious scriptures? Though

scriptures of many religions were preserved by word of mouth, Hinduism probably deserves a special mention where the volume of scriptures is considerably high and the time for which they were preserved by word of mouth also is very long.

353. A realization should dawn on us, that if we don't sink our differences and work together on all fronts, we all would collapse one day.

354. Why should you settle for something less with an omnipotent God !? Ask for the maximum you want without feeling any hesitation. Let him not grant. There is no guarantee that he would grant even the minimum you want! So from our side let us not hesitate to ask for the maximum.

355. What is the use of intellect if they (Jews) cannot live in peace ? It seems in their entire period of civilization they lived in peace only for a very short time. Even today they are always in a war like situation. Though they are successful in making so many technologies they were/are at a loss to know how to make "peace technology'! Jason Buzi of USA wants to create a separate country for refugees with the help of other rich people. Whether Jews comes under the category of refugees according to his criteria or not, he should do it for Jews as well. They are a tiny population and have not lived/ are not living in peace as mentioned above.. They can be easily accommodated in a small amount of space in view of their numbers. .There is lot more wisdom living in a peaceful place than involving in war or remaining in a war like situation 24×7×365 for generations.

356. Charles Kettering told..."Science is an organised way of keeping oneself dissatisfied always". We can never know about the beginning of the universe.

357. It's possible in future that the garbage picker is an educated man at work! Rate of unemployment among educated is increasing.

358. A wise man is one who learns from others mistakes, not by one's own mistakes.

359. There is a debate. Should we give unsolicited advice to any one ? Management experts and some others say "NO.. We should not give any advice to any one unless asked for". But some philosophers feel that, if you think that your advice is helpful to others give it, even unasked for.

360. "The difference between a fool and wise is who gets the information first." Timely and wide dissemination of complete information is a prerequisite for proper analysis".

361. In many places where people have a liberal attitude towards .eating, drinking and making merry do have high longevities though in India –the above way of living is said to be not conducive for a long life.

362. If you are lucky, even your mistakes and imperfections turn to your advantage.

363. I have written a composition contrary to Tagore's Gitanjali, The title I gave for my composition is "Sokaanjali" (सोकांजलि).

Where the mind is always with fear and the chin can't be raised up.

Where knowledge is commercialized and destructive.,

Where the country is broken up into fragments by narrow domestic walls...state, region, language, religion, caste.,

Where words come from the depth of a calculated mind or from the surface of the tongue.,

Where the clear stream of reason has lost its way into the ruthless land of power and pelf.,

Into that hell of shackles, my Bharat maatha, my country is in deep slumber or pretends to be awake.

Be happy and hopeful that one day you will be independent of the above.

May the soul of Rabindranath Tagore rest in peace.

364. It's a law of nature that no one is equally liked or disliked by all.

365. Since prevention is better than cure, better pray at all times whether you're in trouble or not. What should you do when you're in trouble ? Think of both the feet of the God (आपद किम करणीयं? स्मरानीयम तवा पद युगलं).

366. In India the saying...justice delayed is justice denied, seems to have absolutely no relevance. Cases takes decades and we can't expect how the situation/ state of affairs of the people concerned with the cases changes during this long time. Even the cases may take a different turn because of the delay.

367. Around independence we were approximately 33 to 35 crores and now we are 134 crores plus!

368. If you are patient in one moment of anger, you will escape a hundred days of sorrow. One may even may say -a life time's sorrow.

369. One of the reasons attributed for reduced human bondages in the present times is high population.

370. Indians work well, when master is a non-Indian.

371. When you co-exist with people for a long time, high expectations automatically build up.

372. Animals don't involve for recreation—only for procreation.

373. Apparently President A.P.J. Abdul Kalam analysed so many aspects but he had inhibitions to tell them. He simply mentioned, violence, pollution, reckless human action. How and what all he analysed and mentioned the above and what all he meant by that only he knows. Now we should try to understand what he meant. What we can certainly infer is, he sensed something serious. Otherwise he would not give us a maximum time limit of 30 yrs to survive ! Let us give credence to what he said try to understand the above mentioned three factors and take suitable remedial measures.

374. Sarcasm is very dangerous. It can break your relations with everyone and job prospects.

375. Every day 134 crore plus people urinate and shit in our country. Why not to think of measures of conserving this and transform them to a suitable form to be utilized on farmers fields or otherwise ? Green revolution has not only spoiled soil health but also Nations health.. But for the green revolution we would not have proliferated to 134 crores plus population. President Gorbachev by his glasnost and perestroika has collapsed erstwhile USSR while Norman Borlaug has collapsed India by green revolution. Both got Nobel prizes for peace ! But both can be vindicated. Gorbachav could not imagine the consequences of his reforms while Norman Borlaug has warned everyone about population growth.

376. Often Nobel prizes for peace and in literature have invited some criticism.

377. Ask a botanist or preferably an horticulturist. He will tell the various problems of bud blossoming. Some buds just fall off without blossoming; some don't bloom, some take lot of time; many environmental factors affect the blooming and so on. So is with

our dreams. We don't know how many would be fulfilled?

378. An optimist sees an opportunity in every calamity, while a pessimist sees a calamity in every opportunity.

379. Hell is where British are the cooks, Germans are the police, French are the engineers, Swiss are the lovers and all these organised by Italians. Heaven is where British are the police, Germans are the engineers, French are the cooks, Italians are the lovers and all these organised by Swiss!

380. Philosopher Jiddu krishna murthy said, wherever there is charity there is exploitation. If there is no exploitation the need to depend on charity does not arise.

381. Very few emerge strong after facing hard times. Majority of them pay a price and succumb to various extents.

382. To express the power of beauty of face, here is an old quotation....Had Cleopatra's nose been slightly shorter, the history of the world would have been different.

383. In many religions the composition of and translations from the original texts have been controversial.

384. If we are philosophical and attribute our hard times to destiny then there is no problem. We can accordingly live. But when you feel that some persons are responsible for your hard times then it is very difficult to reconcile and continue in life. However best you try to forget it, there is always a constant reminder of that to trouble you.

385. India is a highly diverse country—a tremendous mixture of people. We have no other go than to co-exist with all making compromises.

386. Mark Twain said—."I have never allowed my schooling to interfere with my education". So parents must know how to educate their children.

387. Even expectations built up after a careful and honest analysis of the situation can fail. Either your analytical ability has fallen short or you are unfortunate to become a victim of Murphy's laws.

388. It's very difficult to be true to oneself, because man's capacity for self deception is enormous.

389. Einstein said we are using only one percent of our brain power!

390. It's not only academicians who are going abroad. Huge numbers are also going abroad for supporting services. So it is not only brain drain but also brawn drain.

391. In these days of test tube babies and surrogate mothers we should also congratulate doctors and surrogate mothers who made mothers day possible. U.N. (United Naitons) should ear mark a separate day to wish—"Happy Surrogate Mothers Day".

392. Bachelors (singles ) also must be given ration cards. Strange that no one files a PIL (Public Interest Litigation case). It should have been done when Dr APJ Abdul Kalam was the President!

393. Someone said — Smaller states are amenable to better administration and more conducive to development and it also fulfils the respective regional/sub regional aspirations of the people. Smaller states can achieve better per capita income and GRE (Gross enrolment ratio) in higher education. This is a powerful logic which can lead to formation of more number of states by fragmentation of the former/parent states.

394. People don't want liberation, salvation, God realization, Self realization, Heavenly abode, Freedom from rebirth etc, etc. What they want is a wonderful life in this world ! .

395. It is a matter of luck whether you get married or not to whom your heart belongs. Marriage of compromises are common .

396. Philosophy says extremities may look alike. If in India rape is because of deprivation in U.S. A etc free sex is no more thrilling! Hence the rapes!

397. We may not give up someone whom means so much to us, but nature snatches away.

398. A man said to woman. You see, we men are great. We can speak on any topic for hours together. The woman said, to do that we don't require a topic!

399. Sometimes one's attitude to the problem is a serious problem to others!

400. We are very intolerant towards others for corruption, fraud etc but highly tolerant towards those with whom we identify.

401. In the present time many politicians are commenting on dynasty rule. Dynasty rule is not a modern custom. For ages we have been ruled by dynasties of so many kings. It is a past custom to which people are used to. Dynasty rule is not a problem if it does not become a nasty rule !

402. Russian Joke—A person happened to meet someone and seeing him, he uttered in great surprise. Hey! I thought you are dead. The other person asked in turn. What made you to think like that? The first person replied. Mr. I heard someone talking good of you!

403. The land need not have to breed a hero (es). It's sufficient if the land doesn't breed a villain (s).

404. Roman saying. “Give people bread and circus and rule them the way you like”. In the present times “circus” is an umbrella term under which people have to be given so many things. Otherwise one cannot win the next election.

405. If all are forgiven there is no need for last day of judgment! No work for God on that day!

406. A paradox. Many Indians criticising USA and their only ambition and worry is to see their children land in USA !

407. Politicians have understanding of/ try to understand the voters psyche and accordingly function.

408. Think in this way. We are offering quality education only through distance education (correspondence courses). And not in regular stream! Because, in distance education students get a set of printed notes and a fixed number of contact classes are definitely held where teachers definitely come and conduct the contact classes. Neither happens in regular stream. So distance education is definitely of a higher quality!

409. Once any sphere gets politicized, it’s impossible to depoliticize it.

410. According to Hindu mythology, this is the last of the four eras called -Kali yugam. There maybe brief periods of goodness and a few pockets of goodness in the country. But over all there would be only deterioration with time. This is the prediction of our ancients. Can we work in such a manner to disprove them?

411. “Tell me the name of a great man. I will show his grave.”

412. In case there is a famine, if you give valid money or even Gold and diamonds, no one will give you a morsel of food.

413. Half empty or half full makes real sense depending on the size of the glass/tumbler .

414. Do you believe in Ghosts? The other person smiled and disappeared!

415. Many went to God and complained about their troubles and blamed God for giving more troubles to them. God said. Fine. I will put all your troubles here and divide them equally among you. All of you have equal shares. All refused and just took their individual share and went back.

416. There are so many grievances for pensioners/geriatrics (old people). It is really an indigestible paradox, that we have such a large number of politicians in power who are senior citizens/geriatrics. Yet they are not kind enough to their brethren pensioners/geriatrics.

417. The world says India has a large Hindu majority. It is a fallacy. No one is a born Hindu. Everyone is born either as an OC, OBC, SC or ST!

418. In search of wealth you lose your health. Then, you use your wealth to recover your health and subsequently you lose both your health and wealth.

419. When a Professor was asked how many research papers you have? He replied. We don't publish papers anymore. We directly deal with the patent office. That is real research and that is quality.

420. Al Capp— "Abstract art is a product of untalented, sold by the unprincipled to the utterly bewildered."

421. We talk about so many negatives—scarcity of resources, pollution, hunger, malnutrition, poverty etc Yet the population had been increasing and is increasing !

422. Exceptions or small number of cases do not in any way negate generalizations. Secondly we should have a consensus as to when we can generalise / say "in general"?. Say out of 100, if 80 fall under one category? 70? 60? What is the yard stick for generalization ?

423. Scenes of extreme starvation cases in Sub-Saharan Africa and a Bombay Nurse (Aruna) remaining on ventilator for 42 years, makes one to believe that there is something like soul. Unless it leaves the body the person cannot die.

424. All over the world PhD can be a problem. Hence the following expansions for the acronym PhD : .— Please have degree. Patiently hoping for degree. Probably heavy in debt. Pleaase help.desperate. Professor has doubts. Patently headed downhill. Pathetic homeless dork. In hindi— Paagal honey do. which means let them go mad.

425. French prime Minister Georges Pompidou said. "There are three ways of ruining oneself. Gambling—Women—Science & Technology. Gambling the fastest way of ruining oneself; Women the most pleasurable way of ruining oneself and Science & Technology the most certain way of ruining one self."

426. As we do not have the same social freedom as in developed west, marriage should take a priority over career.

427. Once it seems all animals had a get together and organized a conference. They discussed the issue of human beings comparing them while criticizing fellow human beings. Snake, Fox, donkey, dog, buffalo etc all have strongly objected to the above. All who assembled felt that they have some code of conduct and ethics while human beings have none. So they have finally passed a resolution— "We

strongly condemn human beings comparing themselves with any one of us".

428. Even a man on death bed looks at ladies eagerly. Adi shankaracharya gave an analogy. A snake has devoured a frog from its back side. Almost all of the frog's body is in the mouth of the snake. And in a few moments whole of the frog will be devoured. At that stage the frog's attention was on an insect nearby—it wants to prey on the insect. That's what men are.

429. At least ten words of Arabic origin —with the prefix "Al" are: albacore, alcazar, alchemy, alcohol, alcove, alembic, alfalfa, algebra, algorithm, and alkaptonuria.

430. As per old philosophy what you sow you reap. But in modern times — you sow and someone else may reap and vice versa.

431. If the monsoon is good the agriculture minister wants to take the credit!

432. Lullabies vary in both meaning and language and tunes in different states, and even in the same region. So some factor other than lullabies may be involved in inducing the babies to sleep.

433. A person saw another person trying to commit suicide. He stopped him. And said why do you resort to this extreme step? Let us discuss the problems and resolve them. Both started discussing the problems and finally both committed suicide.

434. It seems tortoises can live up to 6 months even after their brain is removed.

435. When you are in PhD, you have to surrender your brain to your guide/ research supervisor. He or she will give it back to you only after 5 or 6 yrs or even more either after thesis submission or after final viva voce. Till then you don't have a brain and have to move only with your heart.

436. With whatever you become obsessed you become that.

437. Erwin Schrodinger—War indiscriminately kills people, whereas medical science indiscriminately saves people. Both have no selection value.

438. Globally more than 150 billion animals slaughtered every year ! Even in India it's in millions.

439. There are no good people or bad people in this world. There are only people with opportunities or without opportunities. Those with opportunities are bad people and those without opportunities, they have no other go than to remain as good people !

440. What is right and what is not can be highly subjective!

441. Both the sayings were prevalent in the past. 1. You're innocent unless proved guilty. 2. You're guilty unless you're proved otherwise. In the courts the client and the lawyer on the right side keep shouting to prove themselves innocent or right. Not uncommon that the other side wins.

442. Vast majority of people indeed have succumbed during struggle. Only a few have overcome and became successful. And we quote only these smaller fraction of success stories.

443. After giving independence to India, even before British reached London, many Indians reached London!

444. When you sell a weapon, the seller should be sure that he is not the target of the weapon.

***Wishing the Readers All Good Luck***